Placemaking

End-users provide the most valuable perspective and insights into how public social space should function. Much of the failure of urban settings can be related to overstructured urban environments which determine their prescribed usage, thereby inhibiting instead of enabling socio-spatial performance.

Decisions by urban planners and designers should be made with the participation of the end-user to minimise uncertainty as far as possible. *Placemaking: An Urban Design Methodology* presents a procedure that evaluates the preferences of urban dwellers and synthesises these with the planning specialist's expertise, better representing all views. Derek Thomas adopts the Sondheim methodology where cultural clues are linked in a matrix with planning primers which in turn are extended into appropriate planning actions.

A unique new tool for planning authorities, urban designers and planners, this book emphasises the importance of the community while taking into account the expertise of the specialists in creating public spaces.

Derek Thomas holds a master's degree in Environmental Science from Cape Town University, South Africa. His research into the design and planning of socially responsive urban space has explored a methodology that engages all stakeholders. He trained at the Oxford School of Architecture, UK, and is a published author on architecture and urban design.

Routledge Research in Planning and Urban Design

Series editor: Peter Ache

Radboud University, Nijmegen, Netherlands

Routledge Research in Planning and Urban Design is a series of academic monographs for scholars working in these disciplines and the overlaps between them. Building on Routledge's history of academic rigour and cutting-edge research, the series contributes to the rapidly expanding literature in all areas of planning and urban design.

Brand-driven City Building and the Virtualizing of Space
Alexander Gutzmer

Deconstructing Placemaking
Mahyar Arefi

The Empty Place
Democracy and public space
Teresa Hoskyns

Dealing with Deindustrialization
Adaptive resilience in American Midwestern regions
Margaret Cowell

Public Space and Relational Perspectives
New challenges for architecture and planning
Chiara Tornaghi and Sabine Knierbein

Heteroglossic Asia
The transformation of urban Taiwan
Francis Chia-Hui Lin

Building the Inclusive City
Theory and practice for confronting urban segregation
Nilson Ariel Espino

The Robust City
Tony Hall

Planning Urban Places
Self-organising places with people in mind
Mary Ganis

Planning for the Material World
Laura Lieto and Robert Beauregard

Planning and Citizenship
Luigi Mazza

Paris under Construction
Building sites and urban transformation in the 1960s
Jacob Paskins

Territorial Governance across Europe
Pathways, practices and prospects
Peter Schmitt and Lisa Van Well

Actor Networks of Planning
Exploring the influence of ANT
Yvonne Rydin and Laura Tate

Neoliberal Spatial Governance
Philip Allmendinger

Placemaking
An urban design methodology
Derek Thomas

Placemaking

An Urban Design Methodology

Derek Thomas

NEW YORK AND LONDON

First published 2016
by Routledge
711 Third Avenue, New York, NY 10017

and by Routledge
2 Park Square, Milton Park, Abingdon, Oxon OX14 4RN

Routledge is an imprint of the Taylor & Francis Group, an informa business

Library of Congress Cataloging in Publication Data
Names: Thomas, Derek, 1940– author.
Title: Placemaking : an urban design methodology / Derek Thomas.
Description: New York : Routledge, 2016. |
Series: Routledge research in planning and urban design | Includes bibliographical references and index.
Identifiers: LCCN 2015044003| ISBN 9781138124509 (hardcover) | ISBN 9781315648125 (ebook)
Subjects: LCSH: City planning—Social aspects. | City planning—Citizen participation.
Classification: LCC HT166.T445 2016 | DDC 307.1/216—dc23
LC record available at http://lccn.loc.gov/2015044003

ISBN: 978-1-138-12450-9 (hbk)
ISBN: 978-1-315-64812-5 (ebk)

Typeset in Sabon
by Keystroke, Station Road, Codsall, Wolverhampton

Contents

Illustrations

Figures

Images

Preface

How this book is structured

Beginning with a description of available urban design and planning tools and the need for methodologies that engage with the stakeholders in Chapter One, a discourse follows that lists universally recognised perceptions of quality that characterise urban space and suggests the means for democratising the urban design process. In Chapter Two, cultural clues, discernible in typical settlement patterning and urban environments globally, are decoded for their correlation with the urban dwellers' expectations in terms of urban social space. The main focus, the matrix methodology developed by Sondheim, is introduced in Chapter Three as a valid urban design and planning tool, using entries from a spreadsheet format that links spatial performance goals with planning directives or primers. Chapter Four is a description of the spatial performance goals in greater depth and their distillation before their introduction into the actual matrix methodology. In Chapter Five, the facilitation of the methodology is described step by step, and is illustrated with templates for both standardised and unstandardised scoring systems. The operation of the matrices in a hypothetical situation is described to deliver a ranking by importance of planning primers to inform a typical urban design and planning brief. A selection of important principles for placemaking in Chapter Six is a philosophical introduction preceding Chapter Seven, where a linking is suggested between the planning primers derived from the methodology and normal planning actions. To conclude, a discourse on the ethical imperative applicable to all who shape the urban space proposes a value system for sustainable urban and natural environments. In Appendix 3, prototypical environmental specifications for construction work on existing or green and brownfield urban sites are outlined for incorporation into planning briefs.

Acknowledgements

The author corresponded some years ago with Professor Mark Sondheim, requesting his interpretation on the adaptation of his matrix methodology to the field of urban design and planning. Professor Sondheim's response was encouraging, and he also offered his assistance in a process where his methodology would be put to the test in a different application. His endorsement of the use of his methodology for this purpose is greatly appreciated. Professor Sondheim served in the surveys and mapping branch of British Columbia's Ministry of Environment, Lands and Parks. He was head of the Geomatics Unit, and at the same time Adjunct Associate Professor in the Department of Geography, University of Victoria, British Columbia. He designed the matrix methodology for environmental impact assessment, which was published as an article in the *Journal of Environmental Management* in 1978 and aroused wide interest, with requests for reprints and additional information from over fifty countries. He later worked in pedology, geomorphology, image analysis, geographic information systems, geographic exchange standards and other related areas. Professor Sondheim's academic background (Ph.D., MA, B.Sc.) is in the earth sciences, and in addition to his adjunct associate professor role at the University of Victoria he served as a research associate at the Université Laval for many years. His specialties include requirements assessment, programme development and project management, particularly pertaining to geospatial initiatives. His other interests include geospatial standards, geospatial intelligence and spatial analytics. He is currently working at Refractions Research in Victoria, British Columbia, as a senior consultant.

I am indebted to two specialists who have endorsed the main premise for using the matrix methodology as an urban design and planning tool, and the verification of its mathematical application.

Dr Brian Rademeyer is an environmental specialist. He holds a degree in Landscape Architecture, a Masters in Geography and Environmental Management, and a Ph.D. in Geotechnical Engineering. His experience includes environmental impact assessments, scoping reports and compiling environmental management programmes for a variety of engineering and mineral resource projects. Dr Rademeyer has worked as an environmental specialist in Australia, Mozambique, Lesotho and, more recently, Saudi Arabia. In Lesotho he held the position of lead environmental specialist on a large health infrastructure development project, where he designed and implemented a comprehensive system for integrating and ensuring compliance with environmental, social and health and safety indicators and requirements.

Dr Geoffrey Yeo B.Sc. (Hons.), Ph.D. (University of the Witwatersrand) worked as a laboratory technician and was a senior chemist for Anglo American in their research laboratories at Crown Mines, Johannesburg. After obtaining his doctorate, and up to his retirement in 2004, he held the post of Senior Lecturer in Physical Chemistry at the Technikon Witwatersrand (now the University of Johannesburg). He is currently a mathematics and science teacher at a private high school.

Permissions

The majority of images are by the author. However, permissions to use photographs by Brian Rademeyer, Suzanne Allderman and Judy Maguire are acknowledged with much appreciation.

Introduction

Cultural transformations in the face of the major population, political and technological shifts being experienced around the globe are well documented. However, due to the subjective nature of cultural change, democratising the decision-making process in the planning and design of urban space without engaging all stakeholders and role-players is difficult to achieve. Failed urban settings can be related to over-structured urban environments that deterministically prescribe usage, thereby constraining, not enabling, socio-cultural performance. Planners of urban settings are aware that they are planning for uncertainty in behaviourial terms and generally risk failure. In many instances, this can be attributed to the challenge to produce better-quality environments within a constricted time-frame or budget.

One solution lies in the creation of what may be termed 'enabling' environments, strongly suggesting that planning decisions by specialists should be made with the participation of the end-user to minimise uncertainty as far as possible. In this regard a practical evaluation procedure is essential where the preferences of the urban dweller can be evaluated and synthesised with the expertise of the specialist. All views will therefore be represented in the outcome. Modern-day design tendencies are expressed in seemingly endless art forms, adding to growing complexity in the creative planning. Directing the focus to the intangible nature of cultural expression in urban space, no placemaking formula is likely to succeed without first identifying the attributes of urban space that could facilitate the designer's task. A wealth of literature exists to guide and inform the designer's brief, from which generally a set of design objectives for urban spatial components can be identified.

Since the rapid growth in urbanisation, and with the world population now exceeding seven billion people, there has been a growing awareness by governments, professionals and communities about how existing and new urban environments should be shaped to meet the needs of the urban dweller. Researchers have explored in depth a plethora of approaches and adapted methodologies to engage with the end-user in the design and planning stages. Some explore the fundamentals of design, to further the success of placemaking, while others formulate analytical models aimed at identifying spatial attributes that address the new paradigms for urban living, and some that determine the attributes of the public space as such.

Community participation, properly facilitated, could provide useful insights and offer direction towards meeting the cultural needs of the community in the ordering of shared public spaces. However, the issue of subjectivity, on the one hand, and the need for urban design and planning expertise on the other, are problematic, unless managed through a process to synthesise an outcome that can serve as a practical guideline. In the proposed methodology, for the purposes of demonstration, these design goals can then be value-rated by perceived importance in a matrix manipulation process. A hierarchy of ratings is thus evolved mechanistically, which in turn can be transposed into planning primers that become the basis for the design and plannning briefs for those who shape the urban social environment.

Where multi-person, multi-criteria methodologies are being implemented, such as for distance-based group decision-making, numerous practical problems could be encountered. Initiating, recording and delivering a meaningful outcome with the participants dispersed locationally (Yu and Lai, 2011) requires a methodology that is carefully coordinated, comprehensible to the layman, and useful for the experts who are commissioned to carry out their briefs to design the urban social space for the end-user.

Other approaches for criteria-weight determination include expert methods, such as the Delphi method, AHP (analytic hierarchy process), entropy-based method, and distance-based methodologies. These methods can be used as effective tools in solving unconventional multifaceted group decision-making use of the aggregation of evaluations first by criteria selection, formulation of alternatives, and criteria weight determination. Where the aim is to canvass ordering by preference, offset by expert rating of criteria, there are however situations where the subjective weighting – of, say, non-experts – is better served through a facilitated, user-friendly methodological framework to record a reliable outcome.

A study was undertaken in New Zealand using child sampling, stratification of neighbourhoods by walkability, door-to-door recruitment of participants, streetscape audits, photovoice perceptions of the environment, and residential location of the participants (Badland *et al.*, 2009). The study aimed to synthesise perceptions relating to specific residential environments. Rather than being pure data collection, such a survey could go further as a guide for the design and planning of the urban social space. The placemaking methodology proposed permits the prioritising of parameters arising from a process that informs the physical development of, for example, a residential environment.

Methodologies focused on theory from the fields of urban design and decision theory, from social sciences to purely expert systems, still require a method to synthesise the data collection in order to be of use in urban design and planning. It is widely argued that increased community participation in government decision-makng processes has many important benefits, yet innovative methods of manipulating qualitative assessment using a quantitative process do not seem to be normal practice. Such a shortcoming in the practice of placemaking of the urban social space suggests the need for a more inclusive design tool inside disciplines. The connection between the purely functional and the qualitative vision of the value of space is recognised by researchers "so that a new mental map at metropolitan scale is indicated . . . based on a system of choices, logically systematised: the organisation of a vision inside a discipline" (Ortiz, 2014).

Placemaking as an objective in the design of urban space is often subject to the priorities of powerful individuals and other influences necessitating a more process-centric inclusive model.

> *With citizen participation, formulated policies might be more realistically grounded in citizen preferences, the public might become more sympathetic evaluators of the tough decisions that government administrators have to make, and the improved support from the public might create a less divisive, combative populace to govern and regulate.*
>
> (Irvin and Stansbury, 2004: 55)

From the research available and practical examples, it is clear that to orchestrate public involvement and to access the wealth of uncorrelated research material in the field of urban design and planning are by nature protracted processes of considerable breadth and depth. Generally planning programmes do not permit the luxury of unlimited time or resources to be spent on what should be considered as essential preparation at the initial stage. In the institutional mind the issue of a budget is often a prime consideration in the execution of a mandate. Invariably a benefit–cost analysis will prioritise resources in commissioning expertise in the appropriate fields. However, a streamlined methodology, such as the one proposed in this book, which engages effectively with both experts and the users of urban public space will by all accounts be considered cost-efficient.

The adaptation of the Sondheim matrix methodology presented in this book offers an efficient framework with numerous distinct advantages:

- Administration of the procedure is easily managed by a coordinating agent.
- The methodology facilitates the transformation of a set of ordered numbers (quantitative scores) into planning primers (qualitative actions).
- No special expertise is required from the end-user, who can be illerate, or innumerate, in order to score the level of importance of various attributes at an individual or personal level.
- No time-consuming debates are necessary to arrive at a consensus.

- It is inexpensive to administer as it requires no more than maps and visual aids to communicate the attributes of the urban space of interest to the participants and matrix grids to record the values from a simple scoring activity.
- It is simple to apply once the planning primers have been derived from spatial performance goals – a normal function in the preparation of a design and planning brief.
- Planning actions that follow can be linked more reliably to the social, cultural and environmental evaluations derived from the process.
- It is politically equitable since it does not require debate to prioritise preference. Vested interests of all shades can participate, whether from a position of affluence or from a more disadvantaged socio-economic position.
- No sophisticated expertise is required by the coordinating agent to manage and deliver a reliable outcome, other than a working knowledge of matrix cross-multiplication method using standard spreadsheet software, such as Microsoft Excel.
- Robust mathematically, the methodology ensures that the outcome cannot be manipulated by artificial bias in the scoring systems to favour some at the expense of others.

While the matrix methodology is focused on informing design and planning actions, the procedure can become a methodology within a methodology, such as that associated with standard environmental impact assessments (EIAs), where public participation is a prerequisite, particularly during the so-called scoping phase.

References

Badland, H., Schofield G.M., Witten, K., Schluter, P.J., Mavoa, S., Kearns, R.A., Hinckson, E.A., Oliver, M., Kaiwai, H., Jensen V.G., Ergler, C., McGrath, L. and McPhee, J. "Understanding the Relationship between Activity and Neighbourhoods (URBAN) Study: Research Design and Methodology." *BMC Public Health* (2009). Available at: www.ncbi.nlm.nih.gov/pmc/articles/PMC 2716337/, accessed 26 November 2015.

Irvin, R.A. and Stansbury, J. "Citizen Participation in Decision Making: Is it Worth the Effort?" *Public Administration Review* 64(1) (2004): 55–65.

Ortiz, P. *The Art of Shaping the Metropolis* (New York: McGraw-Hill Education, 2014; Kindle edition).

Sondheim, M.W. "A Comprehensive Methodology for Assessing Environmental Impact." *Journal of Environmental Management* 6 (1978): 27–42.

Yu, L. and Lai, K.K. "A Distance-Based Group Decision-Making Methodology for Multi-Person Multi-Criteria Emergency Decision Support." *Decision Support Systems* 51(2) (2011): 307–315.

Chapter One

Planning tools for shaping the urban spatial character

Generally governments only deal with planning issues as they affect human rights, more particularly because human expectations are important in the formulation of social, economic and environmental policy. Participation in the planning of the urban habitat, on the other hand, is a sphere of human rights that has generally not yet attained the political stature it deserves, despite being germane to the performance of urbanised communities in terms of their productivity and quality of life. The cultural priorities of the urban dweller – such as privacy, identity, community life, work and recreational opportunity – have not been given their rightful due for the invaluable clues they provide for the planning and design of the urban dwellers' habitat. Physical planning methodologies need to advance beyond identifying goals solely through intuition, and should provide an impartial and rational outcome.

Many methods employ environmental quality indices to measure levels of unemployment, aggregations of income and education or information about living standards but say nothing of use about spatial planning or objectives. "Environmental assessment methodologies in widespread use today can be catalogued into four major groups: the overlay mapping, matrix, index and modelling approaches" (Sondheim, 1978: 28). The overlay mapping techniques of McHarg, published in 1969, became popular since the method relied on maps already available from government surveys, but the definition of some environmental attributes may have been too limited. Often the use of indices can assist towards developing environmental indicators, such as Kreisel's 1983 model, for describing the existing environment, for forecasting trends in environmental quality and for identifying existing environmental impacts, but they are not universally accepted as reliable units of measure. In fact, Craik and Zube (1976: 165) conclude that "few, if any, perceptions of environmental quality indices have achieved the status of standard reliable measures." Such data are likely to be of more use to urban sociologists than designers and planners of the urban social space.

Existing and new directions

Public space, viewed mainly as a shell or container with the emphasis on morphological structure and functional use, ignores its ever-changing meaning, as well as its context and ongoing dynamics between social actors, their cultures and struggles. The key role of space in enabling opportunities for social action, the fluidity of its social meaning and the changing degree of 'publicness' of a space remain unexplored fields of academic enquiry and professional practice (Tornaghi and Knierbein, 2015).

Attributes of urban space are abstract and sentient by nature and need to be related to the performance of the urban space components. Researchers perceive urban space attributes to be universal and invariant across cultures encompassing, *inter alia*, the need for social encounter, aesthetic appeal, identity of self and community, functionality, social amenity, privacy, safety, economic opportunity, recreational options, and the enriching presence of nature.

From a more specific perspective, the relationship between public space and democracy needs to be explored. In theorising democracy as a spatial practice, Hoskyns (2014: 6) explores "the idea of participating democracy as a space practice," and examines "more theoretical aspects of democracy and public space through political philosophy and spatial theory."

Cultural differences tend to determine perceptions by cognitive association. These differences are important factors that should be captured meaningfully in any procedure that is focused on defining planning and design parameters. Whether canvassing specialist or lay opinion, it is important to recognise that cultural differences determine perceptions of environmental quality. Variables likely to affect priorities in socio-cultural preference modelling and the resultant design and planning directives would be influenced by: psychological, social and cultural factors that recognise life-cycle nuances; personal priorities relating to age and sex; economic and physical context factors generally; prevailing environmental attitudes, such as in the developing world; and the political mechanisms by which decisions are made with, for or on behalf of an urban population. It is rational to employ modelling procedures that enable these cultural priorities to inform the design of urban social space in a constructive and directly responsive way.

The methodology presented in this book is an adaptation of an environmental assessment method developed by Sondheim (1978) into a design and planning tool with the emphasis on psycho-social aspects of urban living, or the wellbeing of the urban dweller. The focus is therefore a creative approach that reduces the high degree of risk for the urban designer and planner as agents representing the interests of the end-users, the main stakeholders. There is a significant difference between the integrative nature of this method and other psychometric evaluation procedures, which tend to isolate the specialist from the end-user.

At the heart of the adapted Sondheim matrix methodology is the process of transforming the spatial performance goals (SPGs) into urban design and planning primers (PPs). The urban designer or planner as a principal agent would then be better placed to ensure that optimum norms, cultural traditions or conventions, ergonomics, design criteria or best opportunities are in direct response to the expectations of the urban dweller.

Socio-cultural variables and perceptions of spatial quality

It is common cause that successful urban environments rely on the criteria that govern the urban dweller's perceptions. For the purposes of this study, the socio-cultural variables and perceptions of spatial quality are encapsulated in the following constructs.

Sense of place

From the micro- (individual building) to the macro- (city) scale, the influence – whether in style or functionality – of the urban designer or the presence of a particular piece of architecture is integral to the success of a particular urban social space.

Familiarity with a place in specific urban contexts is an important factor evoking either positive or negative responses. Most cities have their show-piece public spaces, but similarly most have their no-go areas. Before the twentieth century places that *looked* important *were* important, and places of public importance could easily be identified. In the modern context, this tends to be less so. Some urban designers link the notion of familiarity with legibility. Lynch (1981: 118) defines sense of place as: "the degree to which the settlement can be clearly perceived and mentally differentiated and structured in time and space by its residents, and the degree to which that mental structure connects with their values and concepts – the match between environment, or sensory and mental capabilities, and our cultural constructs." In outline, important critical factors in the 'legibility' of public space are: the biggest open spaces should be related to the most important public facilities; and the point of a legible layout is that people are able to form clear, accurate images of it. Lynch (1981), who pioneered the topic of image maps in the 1960s, suggests that there are overlapping features among people's images of places – namely, nodes, edges, paths, districts and landmarks. It would be wrong to assume that every area should contain all of these features. Note that it is the user rather than the designer who forms the cognitive image of a physical space.

The terms 'hard' and 'soft' spaces are sometimes used by planners. Both have a useful function and contribute to the character of place (Trancik, 1986). Hard spaces are principally bounded by architectural walls and are often intended to function as major gathering places for social activity. Accordingly, soft spaces are predominantly landscaped by the natural environment, whether inside or outside the city.

Architecture and landscape architecture should respond to and aim at strengthening the sense of place. Those who comment critically on the spatial attributes of environments for social intercourse believe that the 'notion of place' is largely as a result of familiar associations with a place. Part of the presence of any good place is the feeling that it embodies, of being its own kind of space with its special limits and potentials. This field implies the connections between roads and buildings, and between buildings and other buildings, trees, the seasons, decorations, events and other people in other times (Smithson and Smithson, 1967). Just as each locality should seem continuous with the recent past, so it should seem continuous with the near future (Lynch, 1981).

A place is a space that is distinctive in character. Since ancient times, the *genus loci*, or spirit of place, has been recognised as the concrete reality man has to face to come to terms within his daily life (Norberg-Shulz, 1971). These associations that people form make certain subliminal demands on an urban space for the experience it affords, such as a sense of timelessness. This places a particular obligation on the urban designer or planner to enable bonding of the end-user with the urban environment. A sense of place has a hard-nosed meaning where street traders set up shop. These notions place a particular obligation on the urban designer to recognise the bonding of the urban dweller with 'place' – a dynamic interaction which is abstract, sentient and challenging.

Observers believe that the character of a place consists of both the concrete substance of shape, texture and colour and the more intangible cultural associations – a certain patina given by human use over time (Trancik, 1986). This phenomenon arises from the need for people, as cultural beings, to have a stable system of places to depend on, thereby providing emotional attachment and identity with place. The analogy on a personal level is to one's own home environment. The universal nature of this dependence on the qualities of a particular space places a very real onus on the urban designer. Trancik (1986: 113) observes: "People require a relatively stable system of places in which to develop themselves, their social lives, their culture. These needs give man-made space an emotional content – a presence that is more than physical."

Place lies at the centre of geography's interests. In a commonsense way geography is about places. But the commonsense uses of the word place belie its conceptual complexity. While the word 'place' has been used as long as geography has been written, it is only since the 1970s that it has been conceptualised as a particular location that has acquired a set of meanings and attachments. Place is a meaningful site that combines location, locale, and sense of place . . . Locale refers to the material setting for social relations – the way a place looks, including

> *buildings, streets, parks, and other visible aspects of a place. Sense of place refers to the more nebulous meanings associated with a place, the feelings and emotions a place evokes. These meanings can be individual and based on personal biography or they can be shared.*
>
> (Cresswell, 2004: 1)

Amenity

If embodied physically and spatially in the urban environment and perceived to be so by the urban dweller, invariant cultural needs or performance criteria can reinforce the rightness of planning goals qualitatively and effectively, and offer direction in an urban design and planning brief. The invariants common to most cultures, described as spatial performance goals (SPGs), broadly encompass perceptions relating to:

- The need for social encounter made possible physically and where appropriate within the various spatial components of the urban setting.
- An environment which is pleasing aesthetically from the collective opinion of a specific culture.
- The need to identify with a place and one's own self-identity within an urban place that provides the opportunity for kinship and social networking.
- The identity of the place, which encompasses its distinctiveness of character or the familiarity and the territorial bonding with a place.
- The ability of the urban environment to function successfully as a place or residence, to enable movement, provide social and cultural amenity, or as a productive opportunity environment.
- The degree to which privacy is made possible, where appropriate even in denser urban environments. The opportunity for privacy is regarded by many social researchers as essential for healthy and productive urban living.
- The extent to which safety aspects are ensured in terms of the physical arrangements for both the individual and community-related security and health.
- The physical arrangements necessary to conduct informal as well as formal business and ways of generating livelihoods.
- The opportunity for spontaneous and formal recreation and entertainment as enhancing factors in the urban experience.
- The degree to which access to nature through an open space system is facilitated – the extent to which the natural setting has been utilised to enhance the experience of urban life.

To demonstrate the methodology presented in this book, the above universal needs of the urban dweller will be adopted. However, in real situations, a community's collective preference should be canvassed in 'visioning workshops' or similar, as promoted by UN-Habitat and other community-based organisations and expressed as the SPGs. In turn, the SPGs become catalysts suggesting familiar planning primers (PPs), as in a typical design and planning brief.

After being linked to the PPs using the Spreadsheet (Figure 3.1) in Chapter Three, the listed SPGs are defined in more detail in Chapter Four. The descriptors thus derived become the coordinates in the matrix methodology in Chapter Five. In Chapter Six the PPs are translated into familiar planning and design actions. The transformation of data from the preference polling into PPs and finally into planning actions completes the process.

Democratising the urban design process

The art of participatory placemaking can be seen as "civil society being engaged by local governments to envision in abstract the attributes of urban social space that meet the aspirations of the prime stakeholders, the end-users" (UN-Habitat for a Better Urban Future, 2012). The disciplines of urban design, planning and architecture would thereby be better equipped to bring their expertise to bear on tangible and more harmonious and enabling urban landscapes.

To inform the shapers of our urban environment, stakeholders should be brought together to develop a shared image of what they want for the public space that they occupy once they have left their own private environments. Precedent will show that there is a strong connection between this shared image and the quality of life to which a community aspires. In effect, the product of this interactive engagement could influence the quality of the community's urban life on a sustainable basis.

To engage with the community and potential stakeholders, UN-Habitat (mandated by the UN General Assembly in 1978) advocates 'visioning' workshops to address the issues of urban growth. Professionally facilitated, these workshops are able to tap into the collective vision of a community. In the initial stages the net should be thrown wide in order to establish the broadest perspective. Accepting differing agendas from visioning participants should not be considered counter-productive but should rather be seen as widening the boundaries of creative thought.

> *Everyone has the right to live in a great place. More importantly, everyone has the right to contribute to making the place where they already live great.*
>
> (Fred Kent in PPS, 2015)

A prime objective of the visioning workshops to achieve a meaningful outcome is to educate as well as to network. Facilitation is key, whether participation is confined to an urban community or widened to include urban design and planning professionals. The presence of the latter at such workshops could potentially detract from the subjectivity of the ordinary residents whose perceptions form the actual purpose of the workshops. Depending on the capacity of the lay participants, information should be presented visually rather than verbally, to enable ideas to be presented, preferably in a non-verbal way. To encourage the group dynamic, there could be merit in holding such workshops outside the home base, which may be a distraction if it is an undesirable neighbourhood.

The recording and documentation of specific aspirations that emerge should be encapsulated under headings, such as 'Social Needs' or 'Reflecting Cultural Preference'. Enabling urban environments and issues of safety, the need for privacy and social interaction within the social space, *inter alia*, are abstract notions that need to find spatial expression. The task of the urban designer and planner is greatly assisted by the invaluable insights that can be gained in this way from end-users.

The boundaries of the urban social space components need to be defined and workshopped separately: for example, the main street, the street corner, the open space between buildings, the building/street interface, the shared court, the primary street system, natural features and private open space. Although these components form parts of the whole, their attributes differ and are defined by specific design and planning parameters. A long-term view should be encouraged with specific time-frames in mind.

The final data capture of such visioning workshops requires a systematic method to process the resulting priorities of the end-users, graphically co-ordinated with parameters from an urban design and planning perspective. The matrix methodology presented in this book is founded on a process to achieve such a holistic outcome.

Precedents to be found in other cities can provide the essence for spatial configuration that contribute to their success through mandated negotiations with stakeholders at all levels. For example, a city's hosting of the Olympic Games provides the opportunity for urban renewal, based on the objective of healthier, safe and socially desirable urban environments. Good examples are Barcelona in 1992 and London in 2012, both of which were opportunistic in realising urban renewal projects in blighted city environments. Obversely, cities in crisis could provide the starting point for discussion and analysis of the causes, which in turn offers direction as to the remedy.

Quite often the town planner does not know that in an attempt to create order, he introduces a measure of chaos; or that he approaches some urban problems from a biased and fragmented viewpoint. With his conception highly weighted in favour of who shall approve his plan: the policy-makers, the decision-makers, and people of the planner's social status, the plan often ends up giving advantages to a few people, leaving the large majority of urban dwellers at the mercy of the ambivalent ambience.

Urban planning should therefore be framed in terms of doing the best to coordinate organisational and spatial relationships among urban dwellers who are space users within the city.

Uyanga (1989: 141)

References

Craik, K.H. and Zube, E.H. "Residential and Institutional Environments." In K.H. Craik and E.H. Zube (eds), *Perceiving Environmental Quality: Research and Applications* (New York: Plenum Press, 1976).

Cresswell, T. *Place: A Short Introduction* (London: Blackwell, 2004).

Hoskyns, T. *Public Space and Relational Perspectives: The Empty Place: Democracy and Public Space* (Abingdon: Routledge, 2014).

Lynch, K. *A Theory of Good City Form* (London: MIT Press, 1981).

Norberg-Schulz, C. *Genus Loci: Towards a Phenomenology of Architecture* (New York: Rizzoli, 1971).

Project for Public Spaces (PPS). "Placemaking and Place-Led Development: A New Paradigm for Cities of the Future" (2015). Available at: www.pps.org/reference/placemaking-and-place-led-development-a-new-paradigm-for-cities-of-the-future/, accessed 19 July 2015.

Smithson, A. and Smithson, P. *Urban Structuring: Studies of Alison & Peter Smithson* (London and New York: Studio Vista, Reinhold, 1967).

Sondheim, M.W. "A Comprehensive Methodology for Assessing Environmental Impact." *Journal of Environmental Management* 6 (1978): 27–42.

Tornaghi, C. and Knierbein, S. *Public Space and Relational Perspectives: New Challenges for Architecture and Planning* (Abingdon: Routledge, 2015).

Trancik, R. *Finding Lost Space* (New York: Van Nostrand Reinhold Co., 1986).

UN-Habitat for a Better Urban Future. "Visioning as a Participatory Planning Tool" (2012). Available at: http://led.co.za/sites/default/files/cabinet/orgname-raw/document/2012/better_cities_for_all.pdf, accessed 15 June 2015.

Uyanga, J. "Urban Planning in Nigeria." *Habitat International: A Journal for the Study of Human Settlements* 13(1) (1989): 127–142.

Chapter Two

Decoding the cultural clues in settlement patterning

Physical patterning, which is strikingly manifest in indigenous settlements, probably produces the most useful clues to the interdependence of spatial form and social need. Urban spatial form, by nature complex, ranges across wide variations and structural divergence, such as from very closed to very open patterns. Spatial systems can also vary from visual order to apparent randomness. Randomness, with underlying order, contributes to spatial complexity and can itself therefore be a valued attribute of spatial pattern. Simplicity, as a characteristic in spatial terms, can also be misleading. In cities often the simplest of social spaces offer amenity, enabling opportunity for a host of human activities, from just sitting to walking, skating, riding or plying a trade. The criterion for quality in urban social spaces, therefore, is not how complex their configuration is but the scope which they afford for the diverse needs of human activity in the urban environment.

An examination of examples of urban textural fabric along "figure-ground" (Trancik, 1986) principles can offer useful and indeed essential insights into the social chemistry of organic settlement, but it is important to begin with an understanding of those cultural needs that underlie the organisation of space in the urban environment.

Qualitative perceptions of urban space

Early in the last century, researchers set out to identify the properties in the urban environment and how they are evaluated by the user. Probably the best-known work dealing with such attributes is that of the Gestaltists, who argued that the underlying principles of visual organisation influence perceptions. These principles enable the observer to perceive discrete stimuli as holistic patterns rather than as separate stimuli (Viljoen, 1988: 87). A visibly organised patterning seems to underlie the urban dwellers' appreciation of the positive qualities in built environments. Therefore, perceptions of quality appear best served by the ordering of elements which concurs with meaningful spatial patterning.

A common pattern language is evident in all cultures and it is concluded by some notable commentators, such as Alexander and colleagues (1977), that towns and buildings will not be able to come alive unless they are made by all the people in society and unless these people share a common 'pattern language'. Depending on the degree of intervention of formal planning principles, spaces are arranged locationally in relation to one another with a greater or lesser degree of aggregation or separation, engendering patterns of movement and encounter that may be dense or sparse within or between different groupings. Second, space itself is arranged by means of buildings, boundaries, paths, markers, zones and so on, so that the physical milieu of that society also takes on a definite pattern. Other researchers reverse the order or their interest in the phenomenon of spatial patterning and study social and mental processes through what they term the 'crystallised external projections' of the process. Their findings acknowledge that patterning should be depicted not as a superficial by-product of social custom and habit but as the main product of rational socio-spatial processes.

Randomness in physical patterns can often mask order or meaning and contribute to visual complexity, which itself could be a valued attribute. On the other hand, the essence of simplicity in a social space could offer a range of creative urban opportunities and not be regarded as sterile in any way to the users. An overarching criterion for quality in urban social space is the scope of opportunity and not least appeal which is afforded for the diverse needs of urban life. Urban spatial patterns are culture-specific and therefore, by nature, diverse.

Spatial attributes embodying cultural messages

It is useful to contemplate the physical form of urban space which is in direct response to the invariant cultural needs or performance criteria identified in Chapter One. Some are more obvious than others: for example, the desire for degrees of social encounter throughout urban space is not as obvious to achieve in planning terms and is probably less understood, although it deserves equal rating. Levi-Strauss (1968) in the United States and Hillier and Hanson (1984) in Europe conclude that spatial patterning has a great deal to do with desired levels of social encounter. It follows that urban social spaces work when their spatial attributes allow opportunity for social contact, but fail when those attributes do not facilitate social interaction. On the other hand, most urban dwellers respond equally to another attribute – aesthetically pleasing urban environments.

In the case of self-identity or identity of place, the inherent practice of territoriality is instinctive to urbanised *Homo sapiens*, providing a sort of glue in the development of group and place identity. Territoriality can be expressed in terms of individual and communal physical space and, as it is important to the urban individual, it is particularly congruent to the quality associated with some public spaces. Also, spatial characterisation is important in the identity of a place, which in turn helps people to orientate themselves in the urban environment.

Physical manifestations in a city that has a strong cultural identity can contribute to a sense of belonging. Examples can be found in the ethnic enclaves in many cities that generally express a search for identity, particularly in a city where social values are unfamiliar to an immigrant population. The need for self-identity becomes an important performance consideration in the urban dweller's sense of belonging and therefore in the success of an urban space.

The safe use of social spaces and security of health are two aspects of environmental quality that can cultivate a sense of social wellbeing. Traditional city layouts related to urban lifestyles knew only the mobility possible on foot, or that offered by slow-moving horsedrawn vehicles. Being compact, these layouts facilitate surveillance of the street due to the presence and proximity of neighbours. The fast-moving motor car exploded the modern city's boundaries and enforced a scale that effectively diminished the security offered by the proximity of neighbours. The motor car also added to air pollution, which in some cities continues to threaten the quality of urban living. Personal safety and health are two aspects that influence a community's perceptions of the worth of an urban environment.

> *Many communities or their leaders allow the future to happen to them, for instance by outsourcing the vision to a professional planner or planning consultancy; or worse still, by not getting involved themselves at all. Successful communities, however, recognise that the future is something they can shape, at least within the given socio-economic framework.*
>
> (UN-Habitat for a Better Urban Future, 2012)

The choice of privacy in the urban situation is paramount to an individual's sense of wellbeing. However, spatial arrangements in the city should enable the attainment of privacy in some situations, and intensive social interaction in others. The restorative power of privacy, at one end of the spectrum, and the escape from monotony through the stimulus of re-creative interaction and entertainment options, at the other, inevitably rely on spatial organisation.

The urban dweller is accustomed to daily travel, sometimes over considerable distances, between home and work. Physical distance is deterministic and since it is a physical dimension equated with effort, time and cost, a positive view of urban life depends on how easily distance can be overcome and not inhibit choices. It also depends largely on how the urban movement corridors are developed and in themselves provide amenity as to whether distance diminishes the urban experience. To provide visual relief the indispensable place for soft landscaping, as distinct from hard landscaping, should not be underrated. Movement corridors, if not purely delegated to function, could be social spaces associated with social and economic opportunity and other options, thereby offering amenity value to those who move through them.

Socio-spatial patterning in finer focus

Socio-spatial patterning observable in historical and even in contemporary informal settlement (most often demonstrated in spontaneous settlements) is largely overlooked as a rational starting point for the planning of new settlements. There appears to be a general unwillingness to move away from normative planning and accepted design practice, and towards the more organic morphology. This conventional approach in planning and design can become prescriptive. In emergent Africa today, for example, the informal urbanising communities, the vast majority of which are without adequate resources, incline towards their own familiar traditions based largely on expediency – and they tend to determine their own environments accordingly. The patterns that emerge are invariably dense and functional, compact conurbations. Even in formally planned neighbourhoods various ingenious physical transformations initiated by the occupants become evident: for instance, houses fronting on to movement corridors become opportunities for setting up trading activities of endless variety.

To the low-income sector, the realities of squatting and sharing space are indicators of a logical response in physical terms to the limited resources available. Such settlements generally show strong socio-cultural orientation and could be source of inspirations for urban designers and planners for the shaping of new environments.

Multiple facets of street connectivity in Africa, Asia and Latin America and the Caribbean are accompanied by informality. "The state of streets in much of the developing world is quite different from that of the developed world, both in terms of quantity and quality. In most [established] cities of the developing world, there are not enough streets, and those that exist are either not well designed or well maintained."

Many of these cities "share a common situation of inadequate and deteriorating transport infrastructure; and poor facilities for non-motorized transport (walking and cycling). One effect of these problems has been the further marginalization of the most vulnerable segments of society who rely the most on public transport and cannot afford private alternatives. Therefore, the diagnostic of streets in cities of the developing world should be approached differently where there is relatively insufficient land allocated to streets, the streets are not paved and the sidewalks not well maintained, and street norms and regulations are not enforced."

(UN-Habitat for a Better Urban Future, 2013)

Authentic urban patterning

Societies described as 'authentic' by commentators such as Levi-Strauss (1968) – in his search for a form that is common to the various manifestations of social life – are traditionally found in the Middle East, Africa and Europe. Some vivid examples of patterning occur in the layout of older cities and the house types that are found within them. A high degree of commonality often characterises the society through the dynamics of a way of life or the realities of resource constraints placed on a culture. Homogeneous cultural environments tend to be hierarchical.

Two typical examples of indigenous authentic patterning are the Walled City of Old Delhi and the Old City of Baghdad, both of which demonstrate very graphically the attributes of spatial organisation in high-density conurbations, and at the same time reflect the socio-economic and pre-modern technology capabilities of the inhabitants. These two cities embody qualities of spatial patterning and spontaneous design qualities worthy of emulation today even in so-called evolved and sophisticated cultures.

Although the Walled City of Old Delhi is in a state of disrepair, this should not be equated with the spirit of wellbeing of the community living there. The city is a working example of a high-density, "self-contained community

Image 2.1 Authentic settlement patterning

deriving its great strength from the fact that its structure is a logical outgrowth of viable sets of social and economic rules governing group and individual behaviour" (Fonseca, 1969: 106). In the Mohalla (the residential quarter) of the Walled City spatial pattern is expressed in what an outside observer might view as dark voids between the buildings. This belies the real quality of the environment. Beyond the darker narrow lanes bounded by blank walls are sunny courtyards where private activity takes place. This urban pattern protects the residents with two spatial envelopes before a public space is entered, and behaviour adjusts from first-degree privacy (the interior courtyard) to second-degree privacy (the lane outside the door) to third-degree privacy (the public square).

In Africa, as shown by Hull (1976: 41, 48), the traditional village of a region displays spatial patterning that has originated from "philosophical thought" and the "laws of nature."

Other physical forms of patterning can be more subtle, less obvious and yet equally significant due to the socio-morphic patterning which they display. Hillier's writings on the spatial patterning of the Vaucluse villages of France uses a technique that represents, quantifies and interprets the social origins of spatial design and identifies consistencies and repetition (see Hillier and Hanson, 1984). A practical aspect of patterning is the siting of settlement where geomorphic form will naturally influence spatial patterning, such as in the many hilltop villages of France and Italy.

It can be reasonably stated that, in spontaneous settlement, 'order' and 'meaning' characterise the spatial product of social processes, and randomness is the latitude made possible by a system of order. On the other hand, urban settings created through indiscriminate application of rigid planning or zoning principles might lack randomness by the imposition of 'orderliness', which implies regimentation.

High density – a viable option

Given the numerous examples in cities around the world, it should be generally accepted by urban designers and planners, policy-makers and all shapers of the urban environment that high-density habitation can be a viable option without necessarily compromising any of the spatial quality objectives outlined above. On the other hand, due to the generally inhuman scale of high-*rise* (as against purely high-*density*) environments, perceptions regarding spatial quality are more likely to be negative. Many such developments designed for the low-income sector, for example, have failed at great social and economic cost. Few of the quality attributes already identified can be readily produced in dense high-rise situations, as compared with high density in low-rise situations. In the search for optimum density levels, where high densities are achieved in low-rise situations without any loss of the valued spatial quality, inspiration can be drawn from socio-spatial patterning of more culturally authentic historical examples, such as where the courtyard house predominates.

In the planning and design of the urban setting, the emphasis should be uncompromising in the attainment of enabling, and indeed ennobling, environments. Since this demands a process that is inevitably based on quality-driven perceptions of the urban dweller, a better understanding of settlement patterning that expresses the relationship existing between socio-cultural need and urban spatial form can provide inspiration for the responsive and creative designer or planner.

Topographical context

The flat, rolling or precipitous topography (or the vegetation) of a site should be permitted to lend character to a development. Where the terrain is not flat, the modern compulsion is to flatten it. This is a disturbing development, as it places the site as well as the building rising on it discordantly out of context with the original setting. Using the characteristics of the site to inform the urban designers' or architects' response to the character of the place is often largely ignored. Rome was founded on seven gentle hills, and that Eternal City's 'sense of place' is enhanced by its topographical setting. Arguably, towns where design imagination has responded to the changing levels of a hilly terrain are likely to be more characterful environments. On the other hand, flat, arid sites – even those without vegetation – can provide unique settings for strong architectural forms that assert a powerful visual impact. The pyramids of Giza – rising skyward on the vast, relatively flat sands of the Egyptian desert – come to mind.

Place experience is real, but often not realised in modern-day practice. The demands of time and expedient responses to human needs often foreclose on the desire to engage with the more spiritual qualities of the environment itself. Rapid mobility through the motor car, the fast-food culture, and the predigested media coverage across global boundaries determine a speed of change that overshadows the instinct to develop a sense of place.

Other factors influencing the use of a site should include the optimised allocation of the land resource to the needs of habitation, agriculture and other aspects of community life. Typically, in older villages of Europe, the best tracts of arable soil were conserved for agriculture while the rocky outcrops were set aside for buildings. In another situation a fishing community might choose a vantage point above the ocean to site their accommodation for better observation of changes in the weather, on which their catches depend, and the comings and goings of their boats. Often such habitation, due to site limitations, is dense and multi-storey, with the public space circulating along narrow walkways and even under buildings.

The urban spatial network as a methodological frame

Significantly, in the study of socio-spatial patterning, the physical embodiment of social custom and functional need is largely expressed in the urban movement corridors. In physical terms the urban movement systems represent a cultural fabric, reflecting a way of life of the urban population. Consider the spatial effect that the motor vehicle has had on the configuration and scale of typical urban spatial corridors and compare this with pedestrianised old cities, where the way of life is essentially slower and largely conducted on foot.

In all cases of conurbation the differentiated parts and functions are dependent on a circulatory system without which there would be no city. It follows that social spaces are essentially integral, nodal and interfacial within this circulatory system of urban settlement. It is thus useful to conceptualise social spaces according to the circulatory system, whether spontaneous or formally planned.

Being the physical embodiment of functional need and custom expressed in spatial terms, the components forming the movement are, in simplistic terms, also hierarchical. Some become spatial destinations providing amenity to the urban dweller. All have distinctive images or spatial character, providing the urban dweller with strong cognitive associations.

Taken from the field of evidence, the urban movement systems represent the fabric of communication characterised by a network of spatial corridors segmenting the urban form. A city's structure is the solid and void pattern of its constituent parts. The voids function as a circulatory system facilitating economic activity and places for degrees of social intercourse. It is thus appropriate to use the urban spatial network, which is the spatial statement of cultural need, as a framework on which to hinge a design and planning methodology.

Each of the spatial components of the urban setting, due to its distinctive characteristics, is both familiar and meaningful to the user and therefore has its own universal identity. Definitions of urban space apply to a less or greater degree to the spectrum of urban spatial components. Stylised and broadly expressed in ascending order of scale and intensity of use, these components can be characterised as follows:

- private social space;
- open space between buildings;
- the building edge and street interface;
- the neighbourhood street or square;
- the shared court;
- the street corner;
- the main street;
- the primary street system; and
- natural features.

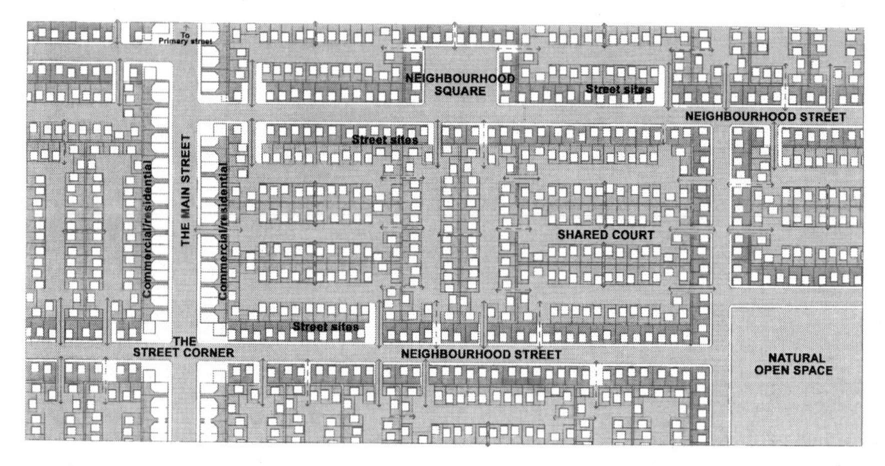

Figure 2.1 Stylised urban space network

By citing such familiar components as a framework, the urban dwellers' cognitive associations can usually be prompted. The spatial character and dimensions of these urban network components should, however, first be defined. A graphic version (Figure 2.1) of the urban spatial framework is a stylised illustration of the context of these typical components within an urban setting.

Private social space

Exclusive space offering restricted access to the public – part of the home environment or shared social space of a residential apartment grouping. Varying degrees of privacy are possible.

Open space between buildings

These external spaces form an uninterrupted continuum of space within the urban fabric – essentially residual spaces that can significantly detract from the quality of the other spatial components if ignored in planning and design. Such spaces, representing an interface between neighbours, are as important as, for instance, the street, as places for spontaneous and voluntary communication between people.

The building edge and street interface

The quality of social spaces is largely dependent on the contribution of the 'building edge' related to the architecture of any enclosing building. This could take many forms, such as arcaded pavements, canopies, verandas, awnings or simply recessed façades. The care taken with the relationship of a building to its open space setting will determine the potential social usage of the immediate environs. The aesthetic appeal of an urban setting is dependent on the visual attractiveness of the building frontages on to the open space. A building that offers nothing to the social space sterilises the environs. The amenity value that building frontages contribute to the quality of the immediate urban space should not be understated.

The neighbourhood street or square

Neighbourhood streets serve not only as circulation links with a defined role for entry to private properties. Squares are feature elements in the urban fabric. As part of a hierarchy of movement corridors, the neighbourhood street or square, walled by buildings, open gardens or fences, provides the neighbourhood with its place identity or a community with self-identity.

The shared court

The global urbanisation of the masses has brought into being urban planning solutions that are becoming more common. Among others, the clustering of buildings around a semi-private shared court facilitates a tighter urban fabric, and provides for surveillance of a shared space by the cluster residents themselves. The court provides a communal play space for children where pedestrians take precedence over the motor car.

The street corner

As the confluence of both vehicle and pedestrian movement, such social spaces are usually more intensively trafficked than others and are characterised by the opportunity provided for more intense social encounters and for heightened commercial activity. Each road junction is a well-defined 'place' – its scale and form and full potential depend on the location of the streets in the urban hierarchy. At secondary level a corner can invite relaxation and serve as a meeting place (for instance, on a bench under a tree) or as a site for informal trading. At primary level the street corner can open into a central square surrounded by public institutions, or become the commercial trading node of a town or city.

The main street

The main street is traditionally recognised for its distinctive social role in neighbourhoods or small-town life. As a meeting place and potential source of community pride, the main street constitutes a centre of activity, culture, education, social intercourse and commerce. With the opportunity for social encounters it offers and the strong identity it presents, it could heighten the sense of attachment and thus a sense of belonging in the community.

A greater volume of pedestrian traffic shares the space with a high degree of access for vehicles, particularly public transport, which is congruent with its efficiency as a movement corridor.

The primary street system

The urban infrastructure usually provides for a major movement system to serve as a link with the wider network of the city or town and to other neighbourhoods. Primary streets are capable of sustaining the flow of a large volume of vehicles and provide cross-urban interaction. Their scale and facilities are related to the needs of vehicles rather than people. For the movement of goods and people, primary streets must be functionally efficient, but they may contribute to the visual quality of the urban spatial network through the use of appropriate design features and appropriate landscaping.

> *In a city the street must be supreme. It is the first institution of the city. The street is a room by agreement, a community room, the walls of which belong to the donors, dedicated to the city for common use. Its ceiling is the sky. Today, streets are disinterested movements not at all belonging to the houses that front them. So you have no streets. You have roads, but you have no streets.*
>
> (Louis Kahn, quoted in PPS, n.d.)

Natural features

Natural features, at a variety of scales, add visual quality to the urban environment. Soft landscaping in verges along motorways and streets with appropriate plants and trees facilitate the movement of urban animals between habitat islands. Parks and sports grounds, golf courses and uncultivated nature add significantly to the quality of the public realm and add to the sense of wellbeing of the urban dweller.

The above stylised version of the urban spatial framework is based on observed patterns in typical urban morphology; however, invariably, the components are not so absolutely defined. For the urban dweller, employing familiar spatial components should assist in the visualisation of their distinctive functions and the opportunities they present in terms of socio-cultural amenity. For the experts, a spatial syntax could be developed to inform design and planning briefs.

For the methodology presented in this book, the components of the urban spatial framework provide the basis for focused procedures, although the notion of the 'whole is the sum of the parts' should underscore the final outcome.

References

Alexander, C., Ishikawa, S. and Silverstein, M. *A Pattern Language* (New York: Oxford University Press, 1977).

Fonseca, R. "The Walled City of Old Delhi." In P. Oliver (ed.), *Shelter and Society* (London: Barrie & Jenkins, 1969).

Hillier, B. and Hanson, J. *The Social Logic of Space* (Cambridge: Cambridge University Press, 1984).

Hull, R.W. *African Cities and Towns before the European Conquest* (New York: Norton & Co., 1976).

Levi-Strauss, C. *Structural Anthropology* (Middlesex: Penguin, 1968).

Project for Public Spaces (PPS). "Reimagining Our Streets as Places: From Transit Routes to Community Roots" (n.d.). Available at: www.pps.org/reference/reimagining-our-streets-as-places-from-transit-routes-to-community-roots/, accessed 19 July 2015.

Trancik, R. *Finding Lost Space* (New York: Van Nostrand Reinhold Co., 1986).

UN-Habitat for a Better Urban Future. "Visioning as a Participatory Planning Tool" (2012). Available at: http://led.co.za/sites/default/files/cabinet/orgname-raw/document/2012/better_cities_for_all.pdf, accessed 15 June 2015.

UN-Habitat for a Better Urban Future. "Streets as Public Spaces and Drivers of Urban Prosperity" (2013). Available at: http://unhabitat.org/books/streets-as-public-spaces-and-drivers-of-urban-prosperity/, accessed 21 June 2015.

Viljoen, H. "Psycho-ecological Phenomena: Privacy, Personal Space and Territoriality." In L. Steg, A.E. van den Berg and J.I.M. de Groot (eds), *Environmental Psychology : An Introduction* (Johannesburg: Lexicon, 1988).

Chapter Three

The Sondheim methodology

The methodology developed by Sondheim (1978), which is presented as a matrix methodology in this book, has the potential to incorporate both specialist and lay opinion to rank by importance the attributes of a public space (expressed as spatial performance goals – SPGs) from the perspective(s) of either role-player. In the process, as is demonstrated in more detail in Chapter Five, the end-user of the public space is empowered to exert meaningful influence on planning decisions (expressed as planning primers – PPs), where this impartial and algorithmic matrix procedure, using simple mathematical manipulation, is carried out. In Chapter Six the planning and design primers thus derived are transformed into a hierarchy of typical planning actions to inform an urban design or planning brief.

Although the methodology's original use in environmental assessment has been demonstrated by Sondheim in numerous contexts, including where the effects of an action are potentially destructive, the method can be equally applied to a constructive process: that of enabling the urban dweller, the interested and affected party, to assert real influence on decisions up to and including the stage where planning and design parameters are set.

According to the Sondheim method, evaluation is enabled to incorporate a large number of project alternatives, direct public participation in an assessment process, and apply to a wide variety of situations simultaneously. The methodology is a useful tool for consensus-building in a wide range of scenarios, and effective at reducing a great many possibilities to a much more manageable number.

The proposed application of the methodology in this book, as distinct from other applications, is aimed at specific urban design and planning goals:

- To present systematically and simultaneously relate the SPGs to the various components of the urban space network, or the interstitial spaces of the urban environment.

- To present the variable socio-cultural needs of the urban dweller in relation to SPGs.
- To correlate SPGs directly with PPs.
- To allow the expert ratings by specialists to be synthesised with empirically derived gradings by laymen for spatial performance expectations where literacy is not essential.
- And to derive a hierarchy of urban design and planning primers through an impartial polling procedure.

The two constructs, the SPGs and the PPs, form the main ingredients in the matrices. The eventual outcome is derived from a normalised, integrated and systematically modelled process by means of the matrix manipulation procedure that minimises the time spent on as well as the expense of a project. Microsoft Excel or equivalent software could be used for this.

The Spreadsheet linking SPGs to PPs and planning actions

To set up the matrix entries, a spreadsheet format (Figure 3.1) simplifies establishing the link between the variable socio-cultural needs of the urban dweller, on the one hand, and urban SPGs, on the other. Using the same spreadsheet, the SPGs thus derived can more easily be associated with PPs.

The empowering methodology presented and adapted to the urban planning process is probably the closest to democratic decision-making that can be achieved while side-stepping endless debate and the possibility of the outcome being skewed by other agendas.

Furthermore, Sondheim (1978), the author of the methodology, states that:

- The method could work very well with GIS systems, because of the ease of generating a number of scenarios with such systems. Such integration may be worth pursuing.
- The method, with or without GIS, might be part of a consensus-building process. That is, instead of looking at the method as a means of deriving a final solution, it may be part of a larger exercise.
- Running independent assessments with different groups of people might be of value, if time allows.

To set up the methodology, the two main variables that have been profiled in the Spreadsheet (Figure 3.1) – the SPGs, of which there are ten (I to X), and the PPs, of which there are thirty (1 to 30) – become the coordinates of the matrices. With proper facilitation, the matrix (Figure 3.2) is ready for presentation to the community and specialists for their preference gradings in terms of weightings and ratings, respectively.

Universal socio-cultural needs	Spatial performance goals (SPGs)	Planning primers (PPs)
Spontaneous interaction Choice of shelter Comfort and amenity Stimulating/drive-inducing settings Visual harmony Sense of belonging Cultural symbolism Promotion of self- and group identity Attachment to 'place' Ease of mobility Multifunctional character Optimum land use/dedicated space Optimum social networking/density Inviting and enabling urban social spaces Facilitated social interaction Personal space Escape from urban stress Degrees of publicness Right to healthy spaces Right to security Right to safe transit Built-in security/neighbourhood watch Income-deriving options Sites for informal trading Sites for formal trading Access to markets Spontaneous recreation Organised recreation Passive entertainment Mitigate geomorphic change Strengthen the ecological base Integrate natural regimes Employ biogeographical principles Enrich urban living with access to nature Affordability	I: SOCIAL ENCOUNTER II: AESTHETIC APPEAL III: CULTURAL IDENTITY IV: FUNCTIONALITY V: SOCIAL AMENITY VALUE VI: PRIVACY VII: SAFETY VIII: ECONOMIC OPPORTUNITY IX: RECREATIONAL OPTIONS X: URBAN ECOLOGY	**1. Spatial continuity** **2. Pedestrian density** **3. Pedestrian streets** **4. Places to linger** **5. Sun/wind controls** **6. Colour/texture** **7. Sensory stimuli** **8. Proportions** **9. Human-related scale** **10. Visual order** **11. Structured space** **12. Sense of place** **13. Cultural identity** **14. Efficient mobility** **15. Functionality** **16. Optimise density** **17. Building interfaces** **18. Accessibility** **19. Sense of ownership** **20. Neighbourhood scale** **21. Territorial needs** **22. Pollution-free space** **23. Monitoring measures** **24. Street vending space** **25. Nodes of activity** **26. Outdoor activities** **27. Integrate nature** **28. Biogeography** **29. Geomorphic impacts** **30. Benefit–cost ratio**

Figure 3.1 The Spreadsheet

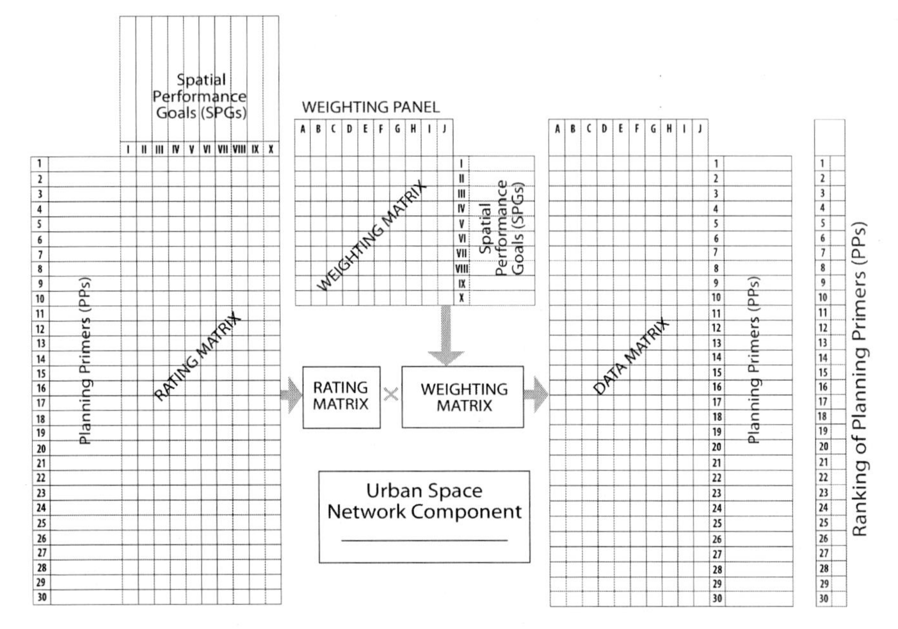

Figure 3.2 Standard matrix configuration for SPGs and PPs coordinates

The methodology is suitable for a time- and cost-efficient outcome, wherever time and money constraints have a bearing. Benefit–cost rating can be accommodated as an item and listed in addition to the SPGs.

Reference

Sondheim, M.W. "A Comprehensive Methodology for Assessing Environmental Impact." *Journal of Environmental Management* 6 (1978): 27–42.

Chapter Four

Spatial performance goals derived from socio-cultural invariants

This chapter aims to elaborate upon the socio-cultural invariant needs that have a bearing on the cognitive perceptions of spatial quality of the urban dweller and distils these into ten urban spatial performance goals (SPGs).

I: Social encounter

Researchers in the urban environment, puzzled as to the reason for the success of some social spaces, and the failure of others to attract and promote social activity despite obviously good attributes, have carried out surveys in order to resolve the problem. It emerges that opportunities for social encounter, in varying degrees, play a large interactive role in the ordering of social space. A very broad application of this notion is that spatial patterning expresses the preferred degree of social encounter identified with the various locations of the urban spatial continuum. This is borne out by Levi-Strauss (1968) and Hillier and Hanson (1984), who turned to the 'authentic' cultures of the past in their research and conclude that spatial patterning has a great deal to do with desired levels of social encounter.

> *The social and commercial role of the traditional street has been further undermined by such Modern Movement design features as enclosed malls, midblock arcades, and sunken or raised plazas. These have siphoned shopping and entertainment off the streets, which no longer function as gathering places.*
>
> (Trancik, 1986: 10)

Over the course of three years Whyte (1982) conducted a survey of the social life of small urban spaces in downtown New York for the Conservation Foundation. Although such a survey could be considered highly location specific, relating as it does to a cosmopolitan community in a central city environment, it has yielded some useful pointers in terms of the social use of parks, playgrounds and city blocks. Whyte also claims that behaviour in other cities would probably differ little from New York, and subsequent comparisons have proved these assumptions to be correct. Also, given the basic elements of a centre city – such as high pedestrian volumes and concentration and mixture of activities – people in one place tend to act much like people in another. The findings – of which those that follow are the most significant – provide a useful commonality in field surveys in other communities and circumstances.

Whyte's (1982) survey evaluated the observations of anthropocentric behaviour patterns in New York's small urban spaces and identified elements that were common denominators in the essential functioning and popularity of social spaces. In the spaces surveyed:

- There was a lack of crowding, despite high-density residential concentrations in the immediate vicinity. Most of the crowding could be traced to a series of choke points, such as subway stations, from where there is a strong 'carry-over' effect to surrounding empty spaces, creating the impression of crowding.
- Sheer space itself does not attract people. It would appear that what attracts people most is other people, even to the extent that they tend to stand or sit and converse in the mainstream of pedestrian flow, where there is the maximum choice either to conclude the communication or continue.
- In many cases children were attracted to the streets in preference to other social spaces, thereby demonstrating their preference for a busy street rather than the available playgrounds.
- Most downtown squares were not used much, except for walking across. At peak-hour midday in sunny conditions, the number of people sitting in the squares was as low, on average, as one person per hundred square metres.
- Standing and conversing patterns show that people station themselves near objects, such as a flagpole or a statue. They like well-defined places, such as steps or the border of a pool. They rarely chose the middle of a large space.
- Of the people who use squares, young office workers from nearby buildings predominate.
- Good social spaces stimulate people into habits. Food outlets develop to cater for the demand, and the space becomes associated with lunch-hour encounters.
- A high proportion of people in groups is an index of selectivity. When people go to a place in twos and threes or use the place as a venue to meet, it is usually a premeditated encounter. Such places then become congenial to individuals.

Image 4.1 Social encounter: pedestrian-only streets

- The most-used places tend to have higher than average proportions of women. This tends to be attributable to the composition of the workforce, which varies from area to area.
- Women are more discriminating as to where they will sit, more sensitive to annoyances and spend more time evaluating the various possibilities. If the square has a markedly lower proportion of women, then it lacks the essential attributes, and more particularly the qualities, sought by women. A higher proportion of women would be an endorsement of a successful social space.
- The daily rhythms of 'life on the square' are generally consistent.
- Off-peak use often offers the best insights as to preferred sitting areas, whereas options would be reduced at peak hour.
- Men tend to take a front-line position, whereas women tend to favour more secluded places.
- Squares are not used as places for striking up acquaintances, and there is not much mingling.

Others such as Alexander *et al.* (1977), with findings based on empirical observation, have developed what is termed a 'pattern language' that describes a problem which recurs in our environment, and then describes the core of the solution to that problem, in such a way as a solution can be used a million times over without appearing repetitious.

I: Social encounter

- Opportunity for spontaneous social interaction.
- Choices in terms of shelter.
- Comfort and amenity.

II: Aesthetic appeal

Apparent indifference to the visual quality of the urban environment obscures the subliminal appreciation of the aesthetic appeal of an urban space.

The approach taken by Shelly (1976) to measure total environments according to human satisfaction is significant and worth noting. Shelly's work led to the conclusion that satisfaction was derived from 'drive-arousal' sites and 'drive-reducing' sites, with the choice depending on the bodily need state. One advantage of Shelly's work is that it has been done cross-culturally and seems to be substantiated in environments outside the United States.

The two types of satisfaction site identified by Shelly differ in their intention as social spaces. The drive-arousal sites include supermarkets, flea markets, movies, night clubs, sports grounds, fairgrounds and other stimulating environments. Drive-reducing sites include places to rest and relax, such as homes, guest houses and the beach.

Heath (1984) also claims that the question of stimulus in the built environment is related to the arousal-increasing and -decreasing characteristics that can be divided into the psychophysical or the perceptual and the cognitive. It has been found that arousal at the psychophysical level is related to the intensity of stimulation: larger or smaller size, brighter or dimmer lights, strong colours or pastels, and so on. The cognitive variables include the 'effects of learned associations' and of what Berlyne (1965) describes as the 'collative variables': novelty, complexity, surprise, ambiguity and so on. Issues of behaviour, interest and personality will determine whether arousal increment or decrement is preferred by the individual.

Image 4.2 Aesthetic appeal: formal and informal social space

Among researchers, therefore, certain environmental descriptors are common for distinguishing responses to the built environment or architectural space. The notion of drive-arousal and drive-reduction is a useful framework on which to develop a discrete planning strategy to suit the demands of each situation. This basis for achieving either the drive-arousing or drive-reducing state to enhance the realm of personal experience will inevitably suggest the use of colour, lighting and noise, either natural or artificial.

Addressing the use of colour in urban space, writers in the *Lexikon der Kunst* (Olbrich, 1987), discussing Goethe's theory of colour, make the observation that the effect of colour sets the psychophysical in motion in the human organism by colour perception. Thus, according to the *Lexikon*, colour perception does more than lead to knowledge about the things of the external world: it may influence the inner state, attitude or even wellbeing of the viewer. Goethe (1970) expressed this in his chapter "The Effect of Colour with Reference to Moral Associations."

Using words metaphorically, 'cold' would describe the commonly held perception of the colours blue and violet, 'warm' the colours orange and yellow, with red and green lying between these two extremes. The lightness or darkness of a colour, which could be termed its 'value', also contributes to the effect that it has on the viewer.

In the context of physical space, there are claims that colours evince certain psychophysical responses, for instance:

- to the viewer, all intense colours seem to be approaching, or appear to be close or constricting; and
- light, grey or broken colours, particularly from the 'cold' end of the spectrum, appear to recede from the eye, suggesting distance.

Such axioms should be treated with circumspection, as texture and changing light conditions could make intense colours darker and therefore not approaching but receding. It should also be remembered that when daylight dims, for instance, red becomes darker and recedes while blue comes forward, until finally it is the *only* colour that is still relatively vibrant.

Colour theorists elaborate on the properties of colour that possess emotional expressiveness: that is, they may appear joyful and vivacious, exciting and activating (especially red, yellow and orange), or they may have a calming effect. Through the spectrum from provocative to controlled use, therefore, it should be possible to create drive-arousing or drive-reducing environments with the assistance of the chromatic dimension and variation. There appears to be a consensus that colour induces perceptions and might influence the 'inner state'.

Opportunities for the application of colour and texture in the context of urban space lie chiefly in the enclosing architectural plane and the horizontal ground plane. Some scope will exist in street furniture, such as lamp standards, seats, fountains and other public space accoutrements. Artificial lighting also presents a challenging, qualitative influence on aesthetics.

The aim is to create a chromatically unified whole, an indivisible artistic unity. Visual perception and content will suggest the way in which colour is used as a means of expression in urban space. There are a few basic rules that it is advantageous to observe and it is difficult to make absolute suggestions about how to design with colour. However, a process in which both rational consideration and a free unfolding of creative imagination could deliver the most successful results.

II: Aesthetic appeal

- Stimulating/drive-inducing settings.
- Visual harmony.

III: Sense of belonging

Urban sociologists say that people need an identifiable spatial unit to belong to, and Alexander *et al.* (1977) examine this need in their search for a formula.

In the most regular situations, the process by which design and the layout of public land has been achieved is a bureaucratic process. Instead, the social spaces shared as common land should be achieved by the collective expression of the will of the people sharing a sense of neighbourhood and belonging.

The manifestation of territoriality is now recognised to derive from an emotive force in both humans and animals. The distinction between self/non-self and group/non-group expressed territorially is instrumental in the development of group and place identity. Since territoriality can be expressed in terms of physical space, it may be considered among other spatial performance criteria. Although Ittelson (1974: 143) views territoriality as a descriptive term rather than empirically demonstrated behaviour, it is nevertheless manifest in expressive spatial forms in many ethnically diverse cities. It is often a way of reducing conflict and of heightening a sense of belonging. For example, ethnic enclaves offer a spontaneous solution, expressing a search for identity where social values are more familiar.

The individual's identity needs are bound up with what Proshansky *et al.* (1970) describe as 'cognitive-descriptive', 'effective-evaluative' and 'role-related' dimensions. These dimensions will dictate how a person will behave and how they will experience subjective feelings about the setting, and where role enactment is associated with a particular urban setting will thereby place expectations on spatial performance. The manifestation of durable subcultures in the United States, for example, combines class, ethnic, residential and religious factors to create a symbolically closed community. Planning for pluralism seems the most sensible way of responding to cultural

Image 4.3 Sense of belonging: shared courts and streets

diversity and could provide the most responsible way to accommodate such diversity, according to Berger (1980).

Borne out by experiments in cognitive mapping, identity of place helps people to orientate themselves. It is useful to explore the significance of cognitive or capsule images of the urban environment, as expressed through what researchers have termed cognitive maps. These are mental representations, unique to each individual, which assist orientation in the urban environment. Generally they are distorted images, and mostly sketchy and incomplete. Nevertheless, they serve an important function since adequate cognitive maps make our experience of the city less bewildering and more meaningful.

Grieve (1988: 195) has found that the amount of detail in a cognitive map depends on a person's socio-economic status and familiarity, and the degree of social involvement with the area. Sex difference and education levels also play parts in the cognitive images. Strelitz (1979) found that less detailed information was presented on the cognitive maps submitted by participants from the low-income sector, even of their own neighbourhoods and cities. This could be due to the the blandness of social spaces that form the background to the urban experience at that socio-economic level, suggesting a significant role for the physical environment in the experience of city life.

It has been stated that the properties of cognitive images correspond to the properties of the environmental settings they represent. Environmental psychologists have a special interest in spatial cognition, as it deals with spatial relations.

In examining the subjective association with place, five performance dimensions for the spatial form of cities have been identified by Lynch (1981), one of which is described as 'sense'. This is the degree to which the settlement can be clearly perceived and mentally differentiated and structured in time and space by its residents and to which a mental structure connects with their values and concepts. In essence, 'sense' is a qualitative attribute and largely subconscious.

Most urban complexes have the ability to evoke images reflecting aspects of the environment. In planning of social spaces it is important to recognise the natural human inclination to assimilate the complexity of the city in a single view as demonstrated in cognitive maps. This process of assimilation of environmental complexities in a capsule image by the individual or group presents a creative opportunity where this human characteristic can be employed to advantage. By designing for environmental quality, and well-conceived physical settings with identifiable features, capsule images could subconsciously promote positive feelings of delight, security and a sense of belonging. The converse is also true of environments that are featureless, bland and lacking character.

Space utilisation research by Proshansky *et al.* (1970) shows that human behaviour in relation to a physical setting is enduring and consistent over time and situation. If we are cognitive beings, as we have reason to assume, then settings have definitions and meanings for the perceiver with respect to his or her role in them, how they should look and be used, which other people should be involved, which activities should go on in them, what they stand for symbolically, and so on. This is true not just for the moment but over time.

It follows, therefore, that settings have a strong identity by association with functional structures and aesthetic distinctiveness. This reinforces the construct of either deterministic or permissive environments as being relevant to performance outcomes in the creation of social spaces in urban environments. Both constructs will establish patterns and satisfy or detract from socio-functional aspirations.

On place identity, many researchers, such as Lynch (1981), see the notion as the extent to which people recognise or recall a place as being distinct from other places – or as being unique – and when form and familiarity work together an emotional response results. Urban designers and planners are often criticised for city squares that are too large. Although they look good on drawings, in real life they can end up being desolate and dead. Kidder-Smith (1954) criticises planners for seeing city squares as only empty areas around which traffic circulates. This raises questions not only of scale, proportion, texture and other aesthetic attributes but also of efficiency.

The association of open squares in a city with excessive vehicular traffic naturally detracts from their usefulness as social spaces. The pedestrianisation of streets in many older cities that were not planned for motor vehicles points to a modern trend that is becoming more commonplace or more reciprocal in the allocation of linear space for vehicular and pedestrian traffic.

Density thresholds have an effect on sense of belonging and, in turn, a bearing on the sense of wellbeing of the urban dweller. Several researchers have addressed the ideal physical size of a neighbourhood, where people are personally acquainted with one another. Lynch (1981) concludes that the issue of physical size may indeed be meaningful, and even generalisable, at the scale of the very local unit. The idea grew in the first quarter of the last century that 'neighbourhood' was the basic building block of the city, and the unit was sized to the catchment of the typical elementary school. But the social assumption of this idea has been questioned. Divergent views have been recorded by researchers and tend to support the thesis that social contacts might be territorially limited to the smallest scale, such as within a single residential block. Otherwise, dispersed across large sectors of the city, the basis would be on kinship, or the workplace, or common interests, rather than place. On the other hand, matching neighbourhood size to 'public power' is promoted by Alexander *et al.* (1977) as a possible starting point. Neighbourhood inhabitants should be able to look after their own interests by organising themselves to exert pressure on local government, which is directly accountable for their needs. There is general consensus that, as far as the physical dimension is concerned, people limit themselves to two or three blocks around their own house when asked which area they really know.

Alexander *et al.* (1977), in their engaging book on the cultural meaning underlying patterns of habitation, identify two important elements in the creation of environments that underlie a sense of belonging:

- People will not feel comfortable in their houses unless a group of houses forms a cluster, with the public land between them jointly owned or monitored by all the householders.
- Everything possible should be done to enrich the cultures and subcultures of the city by breaking the city, as far as possible, into a vast mosaic of small and different subcultures, each with its own spatial territory, and each with the power to create its own distinct lifestyle.

III: Cultural identity

- Sense of belonging.
- Identity of place.
- Cultural symbolism.
- Promotion of self- and group identity.
- Attachment to 'place'.

IV: Functional efficiency

The configuration of all paths of movement in an urban area, which are logically determined by function and satisfy social and economic needs, should invite the opportunity for buildings and building entrances to add to the social space. The architect or urban designer should exploit the context suggested by the configuration and alignment of the spatial movement system. The planner of the urban corridor is therefore, from the outset, clearly involved in a creative decision where likely architectural possibilities could follow the planning process.

Lynch (1981: 118) observes that one of the five basic dimensions of a successful urban environment is 'vitality', which he describes as "the degree to which the form of the settlement supports the vital functions, the biological requirements and capabilities of human beings."

Considerations of speed and scale introduce a level of complexity and should not be neglected in the ordering of movement corridors. Mono- versus multifunctional use of social space has a bearing on the qualitative perceptions of a social space. In an article on urban poverty and city development, Dewar (1984) offers some perspectives and guidelines on the benefits of urbanity. He states:

> when a road is simply a specialised channel to facilitate the movement of cars and other vehicular traffic, it adds little to urban life. When,

> however, it is made in such a way that it accommodates other demands made upon it such as children playing or people meeting and positively contributes to those experiences, it is more than just a road, it becomes a social space and plays an integral part in urban life.
>
> (Dewar 1984: 28)

In the case of poor people in inadequate accommodation, general overcrowding and lack of space are common factors. It is in such situations that social spaces become the settings for community life and form extensions to the constricted private space – these are places where children play, lovers court and older people meet.

Baker *et al.* (1985) observe the street of the immediate residential environment as the child's domain and one of the main contexts for social interaction, as well as for human physical development. This fact is rarely accommodated in official environmental policies, and, although designated play areas might attract some children away from the street, they are unlikely to replace it as the main focus of their activities. However, children are impulsive and often react single-mindedly to something that interests them, which can lead to their neglect of the normal considerations of safety in the street.

Traffic integration has emerged as a major principle in the design of residential neighbourhoods, notably in the Netherlands, where the *woonerf* – or residential yard – was developed. By implication, there needs to be stricter control of vehicles where spaces are shared in more informal, human-scaled environments.

> *The street is the river of life of the city, the place where we come together, the pathway to the center.*
>
> (William H. Whyte, quoted in PPS, n.d.a)

The neighbourhood concept is arguably one of the marked land uses that have shaped the urban form of the twentieth-century city in many countries. Clarence Stein (1998: 150–152) – recognising both the desire for door-to-door mobility and the need to ensure safety for children who wish to play in the street – developed the so-called Radburn Plan for that suburb in New Jersey. The idea of a 'superblock' of residential units grouped around a central green, the separation of vehicles and pedestrians, and a road hierarchy with culs-de-sac for local access roads was extended to a cluster of superblocks to form a self-contained neighbourhood. A group of neighbourhoods would then comprise the city. For Perry (1929), the physical arrangement of the elementary school, small parks and playgrounds, and local shops was the basis of his neighbourhood idea. Adaptations of the concept have proven successful.

Image 4.4 The formal and informal centre city

The issue of residential densities is bound up not only with sociological factors but fundamentally with the problem of optimising the limited resources of land and finance in housing. In a framework for assessing housing options and their density implications, Morkel (1988: 21) observes that the efficiency of land utilisation, the cost-effectiveness of infrastructure and the unit cost of dwellings are directly related to the intensity of the development. Cost-effective planning implies a challenge to reallocate capital resources to attributes that contribute to the enhanced experience of urban life.

The propagation of high-rise housing specifically for low-income groups, in the absence of choice, is considered to be fraught with dangers and potential problems. Worldwide, the experience of high-rise public housing projects for low-income groups has been poor and, in some instances, an unmitigated disaster. Studies carried out in Hong Kong found that people living with non-kinsmen, and those living in the upper storeys of multi-storey dwellings, were more likely to score high on the index of emotional illness than those living nearer to the ground.

One factor identified by Marans and Wellman (1976) that could moderate negative feelings about density and crowding is greater access to the outdoors. Environmental quality varies independently of density and is, in itself, a subjective issue of judgement coloured by the values, preferences and prejudices of the observer. To dispel misconceptions, high density as a planning formula should not be simplistic and one-dimensional but rather understood as a complex amalgam of social, economic, physical and cultural factors.

On the issue of crowding it appears – on the basis of the available data – that only certain conclusions can be drawn and it is unclear that a demonstrable relationship exists between high density and aberrant human behaviours, or between the social crowding of the individual and aggression. It seems that the density connection for humans is very complex, that people are able to adapt to a wide range of conditions, and that whatever relationship may exist is mediated by such variables as gender, interpersonal relationships and social and physical structuring.

Socio-economic forces, such as rapid urbanisation, tend towards accelerating urban sprawl and to sapping the vitality of the urban centre, whereas well-planned high density and concentration of people and functions could in fact enrich urban life. According to Jane Jacobs (1961), street life, in its hustle and bustle and unstructured supervision, can help children to develop successfully, but it is often dissipated into a socially meaningless infrastructure of highways serving suburbia.

Rising costs of housing and services, increasingly expensive energy needs and the pressure on agricultural land all suggest a trend towards greater concentration of people in urban areas. At this stage definitive optima with respect to population densities are not available, so other psycho-sociological factors have to be used to provide insights into behaviour in densely populated urban settings.

The needs to escape from stress and for privacy rank high among the urban dweller's priorities for his or her place of residence. This poses the question as to whether planners, faced with the high-density option as the most viable solution to the urban housing problem, should set out to match people's psycho-social preferences with respect to their environmental habitations.

IV: Functionality

- Ease of mobility.
- Multifunctional character.
- Optimum land use/dedicated space.
- Optimum social networking/density.

V: Social amenity value

Dictionary definitions of 'amenity' are: "A feature that increases attractiveness or value, especially a piece of real estate or a geographic location; the quality of being pleasant or attractive or agreeable" (www.thefreedictionary.com/amenity). These sentient notions resonate with quality of life for the urban dweller seen through a cognitive lens. Some researchers describe urban social space as the 'public outdoor room', characterised typically by accessible green space, small public squares, common land or other social spaces.

In ancient Greece much of public life was conducted in the open air; assemblies, trade, business, exercise and sport, dramatic performances and religious celebrations were all outdoor activities. In describing the Parthenon, for example, Wheeler (1964: 12) observes that the building itself had no inner life, yet it has been described lyrically as a perfect exterior, a perfect piece of man-made geology.

Peck (1982), in a study of life in the Greek agora, notes the incongruity: although innumerable classicists have gone into raptures over the glory that was Greece, little recognition has been given to a very special form of town planning – namely, the provision of an agora at the centre of every Greek city. In the agora the Greeks gathered for political, commercial and social business, and it became the city's living heart. The climate in Greece was conducive to making outdoor life possible, and the external character of the cities serves as an insight into the Hellenic view of that civilisation's social space. Agoric planning is founded on the concept that the individual cannot be in perfect health unless he lives as part of a family in perfect health; and the family, in turn, cannot be in perfect health unless it lives in a community that is in perfect health.

Elaborating on the concept of 'agoric', Peck (1982) makes another association with the 'health' of the individual, family and community – that

Image 4.5 Social amenity for relaxation and recreation

of biopoint, biopattern and biodistance principles of efficiency in town planning. Peck clarifies further:

> A 'biopoint' is a point in the town that the individual must visit periodically . . . Each person's biopoints will differ according to his temperament, tastes and interests; but they include such points as the home, the place of work, the shops, the swimming bath, the library and the running track. Mark a person's biopoints on a map, join them up, and that is his biopattern. A man can have daily, weekly and monthly biopatterns.
>
> (Peck, 1982: 333)

In the Peckham Experiment (Pearse and Crocker, 1943), carried out in London from 1926 to 1950, a conclusion was reached that health is a mutual synthesis of an organism and its environment. Initially generated by rising public concern over the health of the working class and an increasing interest in preventative social medicine, researcher George Scott Williamson at the Pioneer Centre recruited 950 local families who were given access to a range of activities, such as swimming, other physical exercise, games and workshops. Members underwent a medical examination once a year, and they were monitored continually as they participated in the centre's events. Central to Williamson's philosophy was the belief that, left to themselves, people would spontaneously begin to organise in a creative way. This did indeed happen – the members initiated a wide range of sporting, social and cultural activities using the facilities offered by the centre.

V: Social amenity value

- Inviting and enabling urban social spaces.
- Facilitated social interaction.

VI: Privacy

In a paper titled "Optimising Urban Density" for the Institute for Social Research in Michigan, Marans and Wellman (1976) addressed the problem of human response to density and density-related phenomena. They reached the conclusion that little was understood or acted upon by planners and builders.

Understanding the exclusivity of personal space has been the subject of considerable research in this area of human response to the environment mainly in two directions: one deals with people's preferences for, and evaluations of residential environments; the other focuses on human pathologies that may result from crowding. The first indicates that in general people have strong preferences for single family houses on large plots, and home-ownership and private outdoor space are cited as the most important

Image 4.6 Personal space in a tight urban fabric

reasons for their preferences. Commentators observe that although these findings are germane in the discussion on high density, they cannot be applied without awareness of the conditioning influence of other factors, such as life cycle: the elderly are more satisfied with high density since it fosters greater opportunities for socialising.

The second area of research on human responses is concerned with the stress factor related to crowded conditions, which leads to physical, psychological and social dysfunction. It appears that much of the interest in density and human pathology has its genesis in so-called animal studies, where a causal linkage between population density and pathology is suggested.

Noise has been identified separately as a dimension of privacy that greatly affects people's responses to where they live. If there is no material change in technology or lifestyle patterns, future settlements will be not only more crowded but more noise-polluted than they are today, and we may expect more of what Marans and Wellman (1976) call 'person–environment mismatch'.

The need for temporary escape may be met by creating open spaces in the form of sufficiently large parks, especially in high-density settings, where people can choose to find solitude and be away from noise and the fumes of the city streets.

VI: Privacy

- Personal space.
- Escape from urban stress.
- Degrees of publicness.

VII: Safety

An overview of Michelson's (1977: 24) research into the effects of high density on human functioning shows that by examining environmental factors researchers can account for breakdowns in either personal or family functioning. There is a suggestion that high densities only aggravate or accelerate, rather than cause or motivate, any tendency to disorganisation in a personality or a group.

The urban environment is still represented as problematic and complex, a place where civil disorders, crime, mental illness, alienation and general social disorganisation and morbidity thrive. Increases in population densities alone cannot be held responsible for these social morbidity patterns, as many older industrial cities in Europe and the United States have stabilised high-density populations and have not registered a general decline in mental health. In surveys carried out in Pruitt-Igoe, New York – a low-income, high-density residential area at forty-eight units to the acre – the crime rate did not correlate specifically with density but with building height and type.

Image 4.7 Safety in precincts or traffic-free pedestrianways

The crime rate was found to increase almost proportionately with building height. On the basis of the surveys, it was concluded that an increase in defensible space can singularly reduce crime, and that as long as buildings remain low, high crime rates normally will not occur.

By the end of the last century, the Israeli Department of Housing had developed an exemplary programme for high-density living. In the housing of new settlers from the Diaspora in the cities, not only their language differences but their diversity of culture challenged the normal integration strategies for immigrants. To accompany the programme of resettlement, integration was facilitated by resident sociologists, who were placed strategically in the new high-density neighbourhoods. In this way a sense of neighbourliness, designed to promote a sense of security, was immediately established.

The other side of the safety coin is the issue of environmental health. Public health is inextricably bound up with pollution-free environments. Perceptions of pollution arising from uncontrolled urban activities influence and prejudice people negatively against specific places, with a consequent decline and degradation of those places.

VII: Safety

- Right to healthy spaces.
- Right to security.
- Right to safe transit.
- Built-in security/neighbourhood watch.

VIII: Economic opportunity

The creep of suburbia in cities of both the developed and developing worlds has, in many instances, systematically dissipated the productive activities of urban life and frustrated the economic potential inherent in more interactive urban settings. In research into informal and spontaneous trading in public spaces, Rudman (1988) concludes that such a development is recognised as one of the most important to emerge in the developing world.

Image 4.8 Food gardening in remnant city space

It would be remiss to believe that the proliferation of traders in the informal sector of developing countries is unproductive merely because, for instance, ten traders compete where two or three could easily satisfy demand. One near-universal characteristic of this sector is the very low capital intensity. Sunter (1987) observes that another characteristic is the sector's dependence on individual rather than institutional resources.

> *A great urban park is a safety valve for the city, in which people living in dense urban areas can find breathing room.*
>
> *An informal public market economy thrives in many cities around the world, but often chaotically – clogging streets, competing unfairly with local businesses, and limiting the hope of upward mobility to marginalized populations. Markets can, however, provide a structure and a regulatory framework that helps grow small businesses, preserve food safety, and make a more attractive destination for shoppers.*
>
> (PPS, n.d.b)

The informal sector has been defined as that part of the economy which embraces all micro-businesses, many of which are unrecorded in any formal table of statistics produced at national level. Little infrastructure is required, apart from a piece of public or private space with access to the consumer. In fact, the private and public sectors alike increasingly appreciate that the informal, unrecorded sector is part of the national economy and should be treated as such. According to Rudman (1988), this is substantiated by the fact that the participants of the informal sector obtain large proportions of their goods and services, raw materials and labour from the formal sector.

Very often working in the context of the informal sector, due to the demand for their goods and services, small-scale entrepreneurs are able to move into the formal sector. The main trading activities in the informal sector can be grouped as follows:

- Retail distribution – street traders/hawkers, pedlars, water-sellers, firewood merchants, empty-bottle dealers, rubbish recyclers, shebeen owners.
- Personal services – shoe repairs, hairdressers, bakers, witchdoctors, child-minders, gardeners, chars, musicians, car washers, beggars.
- Repair services – tinkers, motor repairers, panel beaters, upholsterers, house painters, home-appliance repairers, tilers.
- Productive and secondary furniture-makers, dressmakers, knitters, crocheters, ice-makers, traditional craftsmen.
- Building and construction – contractors and associated operators, such as plumbers, plasterers, painters, electricians.

Image 4.9 Spontaneous use of unstructured urban space

- Transport – taxis, truckers.
- Accommodation – subletters of land and premises.

A large number of these informal sector activities can take place in the open, in public areas, provided that economic and spatial opportunity is created appropriately to accommodate them in the urban setting.

Flea markets characterise the informal sector trading pattern. A most important consideration is that the physical relationship of the market to its surroundings must contribute positively to the area as a whole, integrate well and be in scale, with impact that is beneficial to all.

VIII: Economic opportunity

- Income-deriving options.
- Sites for informal trading.
- Sites for formal trading.
- Access to markets.

IX: Recreational opportunity

Active and passive options to pursue recreational fulfilment are both important. Social spaces are potential sites for enriching the lifestyle of the urban dweller, not only in the way in which they enable social interaction, but also to the extent that they facilitate relaxation. People use leisure differently. Participating in leisure-time activity provides emotional release, creative opportunity and an escape from monotony. The physical attributes of social spaces, where entertainment can be enacted and recreational options facilitated, influence perceptions of the worth of those spaces.

Alexander *et al.* (1977: 299) note that "Man has a great need for mad, subconscious processes to come into play, without unleashing them to such an extent that they become socially destructive." Unfortunately, the circuses and carnivals known to many cultures are diminishing in number, giving way to the age of dependence on entertainment provided through electronic media and by means of intensive capital expenditure. The situation then becomes both economic- and culture-related.

Spontaneous street entertainment is likely to find a site in any part of the urban setting that has appeal and therefore attracts people. Many towns in the developing world that have colourful street life, based on spontaneous 'unleashing' of the need to entertain and be entertained, are likely to change in the future. It is therefore important that the urban environment should have public places where fairs and festivals can be sited, and that they are central enough to be accessible to crowds. However, recreation takes many forms, both passive and active. Craft fairs attest to the fact that many people

Image 4.10 City spaces for impromptu activities

seek recreation through creativity. Unlike flea markets, craft fairs and open-air exhibitions do not need to be situated in public spaces that are frequented by large numbers of people.

IX: Recreational options

- Spontaneous recreation.
- Organised recreation.
- Passive entertainment.

X: Access to nature

It is no secret that cities experience increasing signs of environmental stress through poor air quality, excessive noise and traffic congestion. Unbridled urban development can ride roughshod over greenfield sites, tracts of otherwise productive land, or areas of ecological biodiversity. Mitigation and enhancement of green areas within the urban context in a sustainable way can lessen the adverse effects of urbanisation. In the developed world, support for more green space in urban areas is evident where traffic emissions, air quality, microclimate, noise, accessibility and social wellbeing are becoming integral parts of planning policy (De Riddera *et al.* 2004).

From an ecological perspective, fragmentation of the natural landscape in the urban environment has resulted in, most often, only token residual islands of vegetated areas in settings highly modified by buildings and hard landscaping. Apart from the opportunity to strengthen the ecological base on which the urban setting is founded, the psychophysical benefit of green spaces is a worthy objective in itself. Particularly in the newly developing countries, people have become familiar with the total annihilation of the original landscape in favour of the 'urban heat island'. The adoption of a biogeographical approach in urban design and planning would enrich the urban setting and thus urban living.

Roberts (1985) identifies a need for a new approach to the conventional framework for the design of urban open space. Until quite recently, little attention was directed towards understanding the natural processes that have contributed to the physical form of the city. The typical urban environment has been shaped by technology, the goals of which are economic rather than environmental or social. As a result, the advancing city, through rapid urbanisation, has often replaced complex natural environments with biologically sterile man-made landscapes that are not opimising development opportunities, either social or ecological.

An alternative basis for landscape transformation, in line with growing awareness of and concern for the conservation of the environment, energy demands and natural resources, is becoming essential.

> *Urban ecology describes a particular environmental effort which takes its point of departure in the environmental state of a specific urban area and in citizen participation, while seeking to develop overall solutions to problems connected with the area's resource consumption, environmental impact, and nature. Thus urban ecology focuses on a given PLACE (a building, a settlement, a neighbourhood, an area, or in principle a whole town) and on a given group of citizens.*
>
> (Munkstrup, 1995: 2)

Image 4.11 Access to nature for relaxation and education

In 1993 the Danish Minister for the Environment appointed a Consultative Committee on Urban Ecology. This committee consisted of representatives from several sectors: the Ministries of Housing, Transport and the Environment, the research institutes and the municipalities. "According to the basic concept pursued, individual steps and measures toward this aim are debated in a discursive process. It involves the municipality, scientific and technical advisors, planning experts, and last but not least the residents and citizens as a whole."

(Consultative Committee on Urban Ecology, 1997)

Where urbanisation is the extensive and significant modification of natural regimes, wind patterns and precipitation – and, depending on scale, even the climatic characteristics of a region – can change significantly. These changes arise from alterations in the natural energy balance due to the presence of buildings and hardened surfaces.

In studies on the energy circulation of the urban area, Douglas (1983: 36) describes the energy flows as twofold: "the natural but people-modified energy flows, powered by solar radiation, and the artificial and people-made energy flows involving both fossil fuels and renewable resources." The city, on a metropolitan scale, can be distinguished as a 'hot-spot' or heat island. Buildings and paved surfaces reflect the incoming solar radiation in a different way than natural earth surface materials. Such heat that is absorbed is essentially short-wave energy, which is later emitted as long-wave energy. A significant difference in ambient temperature between a typical central business district and high or low residential areas is revealing.

Research has shown that temperatures in urban areas are affected by the following factors:

- The high conductivities and heat-storage capacities of the walls and roofs of buildings and paved areas, as well as their ability to reflect heat, substantially exceed those of natural soils and vegetation.
- The three-dimensional vertical texture of the built-up area, as against the two-dimensional planal texture of undeveloped areas, results in a significant increase in heat-absorbing surfaces.
- Buildings with large vertical faces create exchanges of energy mass and momentum.
- Large areas of impervious paved surfaces reduce evaporation and transpiration through the rapid removal of run-off, fundamentally altering the urban moisture and heat budget.
- The emission of pollutants and dust into the urban atmosphere modifies long-wave radiation processes with consequent rises in temperature.

- Wind patterns are altered by modifications to the ground surface and the presence of buildings.

In the planning of a new urban setting, it is inevitable that a process of geomorphological modification will take place. Douglas (1983: 36) elaborates on this process as follows:

- The urban circulation most commonly develops at night during the maximum rural–urban centre temperature difference, when marked ground-level air movement towards the urban core occurs. Aloft air moves outward at a higher level over the city towards the rural areas, where it descends to ground level. The resulting pattern is a circulating system of air newly arrived at ground level at the urban fringe, which returns to the city centre. This condition would be dependent on weak regional wind velocities.
- Although excessive gusts are caused in some spaces between buildings, the wind velocity in built-up areas is generally lower than in open country.
- Streets and open spaces facilitate air flow, thereby improving ventilation and air circulation in the inner parts of town.

Experts agree that modification to the water balance of the city arises from the hardened urban surfaces and drainage systems, which encourage rapid run-off and decrease infiltration into the ground. There is a loss of recharge to the groundwater body with consequent discharge to stream channels during dry periods. Other hydrological effects include a decline in the quality of water and changes in the hydrological amenities of streams.

Urbanisation appears to affect precipitation:

- by increases in hygroscopic nuclei, in turbulence via increased surface roughness;
- through convection because of increased hard surface temperature; and
- through the addition of water vapour by combustion sources.

The effect of development on biological diversity in urban areas can be countered only by planning for the conservation of wildlife habitats or by the deliberate creation or strengthening of such habitats. The obvious place for this strategy to be applied is within the urban spatial continuum. Such a planning strategy would supersede conventional thinking and the culture from which the familiar, traditional landscape and urban parks have evolved, where horticulture rather than ecology has determined urban park development and maintenance. For changes to existing, brown- or greenfield sites, biogeographical guidelines should be developed as an alternative to an uneconomic struggle to suppress natural landscapes and maintain order and control.

Design that favours wildlife habitats is now recognised as the responsible approach to urban planning.

X: Access to nature

- Mitigate geomorphic change from urbanisation.
- Strengthen the ecological base.
- Integrate natural regimes.
- Employ biogeographical principles.
- Enrich urban living through access to nature.

References

Alexander, C., Ishikawa, S. and Silverstein, M. *A Pattern Language* (New York: Oxford University Press, 1977).

Anderson, J.A. *Cognitive Psychology and its Implications* (San Francisco: Worth, 2014).

Baker, I., Thompson, J.C. and Bowers, P.H. "Children in Traffic Research on Post-Radburn Housing Areas." *Ekistics* 52(312) (1985): 247–252.

Berger, J. "Landscape Patterns of Local Social Organisation and Their Importance for Land Use Planning." *Landscape Planning* 8 (1980): 193–232.

Berlyne, D.E. *Structure and Direction in Thinking* (New York: John Wiley & Sons, 1965).

Consultative Committee on Urban Ecology. "Aarhus: Demonstrating Ways of Meeting Urban Ecological Renewal Needs" (1997). Available at: http://infohouse.p2ric.org/ref/24/23445.htm, accessed 27 November 2015.

De Riddera, K., Adamec, A., Banuelos, A., Bruse, M., Burger, M., Damsgaard, O., Dufek, J., Hirsch, J., Lefebre, F., Perez-Lacorzana, J.M., Thierry, A. and Web, C. "An Integrated Methodology to Assess the Benefits of Urban Green Space." *Science of the Total Environment: Highway and Urban Pollution* 334–335 (2004): 489–497.

Dewar, D. "Urban Poverty and City Development." *Architecture SA* March/April (1984): 27–28.

Douglas, I. *The Urban Environment* (London: Edward Arnold, 1983).

von Goethe, J.W. *The Theory of Colours* (Cambridge, MA: The MIT Press, 1970).

Grieve, K. *The Built Environment, Environmental Psychology: An Introduction* (Johannesburg: Lexicon, 1988).

Heath, T. *Method in Architecture* (Devon: John Wiley & Sons, 1984).

Hillier, B. and Hanson, J. *The Social Logic of Space* (Cambridge: Cambridge University Press, 1984).

Ittelson, W.H. *An Introduction to Environmental Psychology* (Boston, MA: Holt Rinehart & Winston, 1974).

Jacobs, J. *The Death and Life of Great American Cities* (New York: Random House, 1961).

Kidder-Smith, G.E. *Italy Builds* (London: Architectural Press, 1954).

Levi-Strauss, C. *Structural Anthropology* (Middlesex: Penguin, 1968).

Lynch, K. *A Theory of Good City Form* (London: The MIT Press, 1981).

Marans, R.W. and Wellman, S.J. "Optimising Urban Density." *The Environment of Human Settlement: Proceedings of the Conference Held in Brussels, Belgium* 1(2) (1976): 123–148.

Michelson, W. *Environmental Choice, Human Behaviour and Residential Satisfaction* (London: Oxford University Press, 1977).

Morkel, M.P. "Residential Densities – Quo Vadis." In *Housing in South Africa* December (1988): 21.

Munkstrup, N. "Examples of Urban Ecology in Denmark." *Interplan* 13 (1995): 2.

Olbrich, H. (ed.) *Lexikon der Kunst* (Leipzig: Seemann, 1987).

Pearse, I.H. and Crocker, L.H. *The Peckham Experiment* (London: Allen & Unwin, 1943).

Peck, A.J.A. "Agoric Planning." *Ekistics* 49(295) (1982): 333–336.

Perry, C.A. "The Neighbourhood Unit, Monograph 1: Committee on Regional Plan of New York and its Environs." In *Neighbourhood and Community Planning. Regional Survey*, vol. 7 (New York: Committee on Regional Plan of New York and its Environs, 1929).

Project for Public Spaces (PPS). "Streets as Places: How Transportation Can Create a Sense of Community" (n.d.a). Available at: www.pps.org/reference/streets-as-places-how-transportation-can-create-a-sense-of-community/, accessed 19 July 2015.

Project for Public Spaces (PPS). "Ten Strategies for Transforming Cities and Public Spaces through Placemaking" (n.d.b). Available at: www.pps.org/reference/ten-strategies-for-transforming-cities-through-placemaking-public-spaces/, accessed 15 June 2015.

Proshansky, H.M., Ittelson, W.H. and Rivlin, L.G. *Environmental Psychology: Man and his Physical Setting* (New York: Holt, Rinehart & Winston, 1970).

Roberts, D. "Urban Open Space Planning in South Africa – the Need for a New Approach." *Environment* October/November (1985): 11–13.

Rudman, T. *The Third World: South Africa's Hidden Wealth*, 2nd edition (Johannesburg: Business Dynamics, 1988).

Shelly, M. "Residential and Institutional Environments". In K.H. Craik and E.H. Zube (eds), *Perceiving Environmental Quality* (New York and London: Plenum Press, 1976).

Stein, C.S. "The Radburn Plan: Notes on the New Town Planned for the City Housing Corporation." In K.C. Parsons (ed.), *The Writings of Clarence S. Stein: Architect of the Planned Community* (Baltimore, MD: Johns Hopkins University Press, 1998).

Strelitz, J. "Environmental Perception: An Approach to Urban Planning." Unpublished dissertation, Department of City and Regional Planning, Witwatersrand University (1979).

Sunter, C. *The World and South Africa in the 1990s* (South Africa: Human and Roussouw, 1987).

Wheeler, M. *Roman Art and Architecture* (New York: Praeger, 1964).

Whyte, W.H. "Small Space is Beautiful: Design as if People Mattered." *Technology Review* 85(5) (1982): 36–40.

Chapter Five

Modelling the elemental ingredients of the Sondheim matrix

Using the Spreadsheet (Figure 3.1) for the main coordinates of the matrix, the spatial performance goals (SPGs I–X), are transposed as planning primers (PPs 1–30). In Chapter Four the SPGs were given expanded definition based on recognised socio-cultural descriptors. The variables would relate to the particular circumstances for which the procedure is being facilitated.

The placing of the SPGs and PPs as coordinates in the matrix completes the preliminaries for the methodology. Either one of two alternatives – represented by Template A (Figure 5.1) for standardised scores and Template B (Figure 5.2) for unstandardised scores – is selected for the facilitation process by an independent Coordinating Body.

> *Be sure to target special interest groups such as environmental groups, but do not neglect to include people who are not part of any organised group in the community, such as homemakers. The visioning coordinating party should make the final selection of participants. One way to collect candidates is an open vacancy and a selection based on expressed commitments, respecting the balances in terms of gender, age, educational and professional background, etc. Another way is to involve one or more NGOs or CBOs and let them propose a selection of participants. Yet another decision concerns the number of people to involve in a visioning workshop. Much will depend of course on the available resources but the larger the group, the better the chances for full representation. However, practice has taught that the best results are achieved with groups between 40 and 60 participants.*
>
> (UN-Habitat for a Better Urban Future, 2012)

The Coordinating Body could be from within a public agency, a private consultancy or educational institution to communicate the mechanics of the process and to select a group of community representatives, possibly recruited from prior envisioning workshops (to become the Weighting Panel) as well as practitioners trained with expertise relevant to the particular urban design and planning project under consideration (to become the Rating Panel).

Four immediate tasks of the Coordinating Body are:

- List the coordinates in the matrix, SPGs and PPs, derived from earlier distillation in the Spreadsheet (Figure 3.1). A degree of pre-screening is desirable if the variables are to be relevant.
- Provide a map and visual material of the specific urban space that is the focus of the process. In the case of urban placemaking these would typically be: open space between buildings; the building edge and street interface; the neighbourhood street or square; the shared court; the street corner; the main street; the primary street system; and natural features.
- Select a Rating Panel comprising specialists whose collective proficiencies cover all of the SPGs and PPs being listed in the matrix. Typically the specialists would be practitioners in the field of urban design and planning. However, further specialisation could be necessary where, for example, 'ecological diversity' is listed as a specific attribute or SPG. Members of the Rating Panel individually rate the project variables according to specific criteria formulated for each of the design and planning attributes. Their modus operandi for the evaluation of the SPGs in terms of PPs should depend on their training and experience.
- The formation of the Weighting Panel, which typically could include public interest groups, community organisations, neighbourhood representatives and other stakeholders. Ideally the members should have knowledge about the project and its objectives, such as a collective vision derived from prior participation in a 'visioning workshop' (UN-Habitat for a Better Urban Future, 2012), and about governmental policies that have some bearing on it. Each member of the Weighting Panel is responsible for evaluating from a personal and cognitive perspective. The evaluations are therefore quantitative in respect of qualitative perceptions, so weightings cannot claim to be reached through scientific distillation. However, the mathematical robustness has been demonstrated.

The use of polling sheets (see Appendices 1 and 2) could streamline the entry of scores from both the specialists and the urban dwellers or their representative.

In order to minimise dissatisfaction with the outcome, the Weighting Panel must find the Rating Panel acceptable. Additionally, the individuals on both panels must agree to the listings that populate the matrix methodology.

Two matrix methodology options

Depending on the scope of the project under review, either one of two options may be adopted by the Coordinating Committee:

1. Where the Rating and Weighting Panels use a uniform interval or ratio scale, where standardisation of scores would not be necessary.
2. Where the Rating and Weighting Panels are able to choose unstandardised interval or ratio scales, where standardisation of scores would be necessary.

In the former (Figure 5.1) uniform scoring is prescribed, thereby eliminating the need for standardisation. This simplifies the procedure yet achieves a reliable outcome. Rating scores of the PPs by the Rating Panel and weighting scores of the SPGs by the Weighting Panel could be on a selected basis, but scoring of all the entries should be of the prescribed uniform scale.

The latter (Figure 5.2) is a lengthier procedure as it demands standardisation of the scores of both the Rating and the Weighting matrices in order to obtain a reliable outcome. This option allows individual panellists to score selected PPs using non-uniform scores. It is therefore suited to a team of specialists who might be participating from different locations. Weighting scores of the SPGs by the Weighting Panel could be on a selected basis, but scoring of all the entries should be of the prescribed uniform scale.

The first procedure, involving prescribed scores that do not require standardisation, is presented below to illustrate the graphic form of the methodology without scores.

1. Using uniform interval or ratio scores (Figure 5.1)

The matrix modelling template should be focused on a specific urban spatial component, such as the main street or the neighbourhood square.

The matrix modelling templates, with coordinates of x and y, consists of two main components:

- the Rating matrix, for specialists to score on the basis of related planning actions as perceived from a specialist perspective; and
- the Weighting matrix, for the urban dwellers to score on the basis of the cognitive importance of the environmental aspects that affect them.

2. Using non-uniform interval or ratio scales (Figure 5.2)

In cases where non-uniform scoring is indicated, for logistical or other reasons, the matrix procedure is similar but requires standardisation to achieve a reliable outcome.

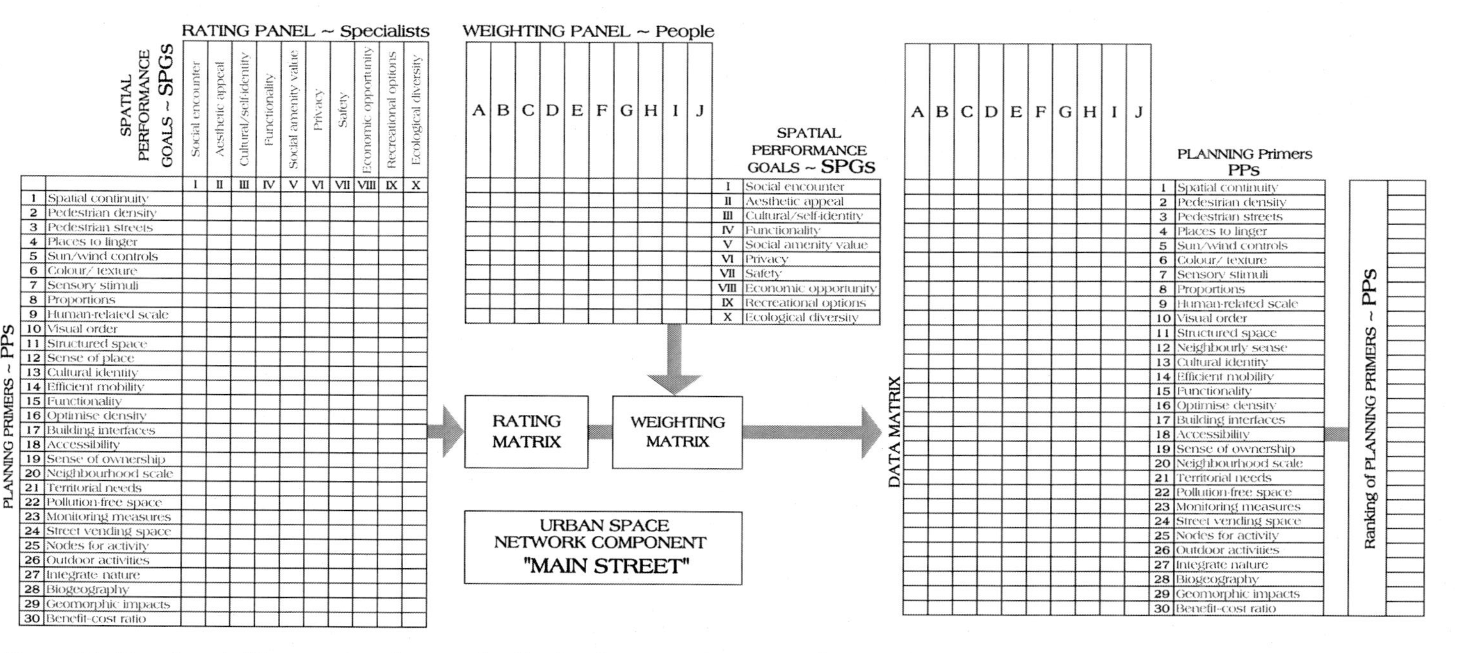

Figure 5.1 Template A: The matrix using standardised ratio scores. Step one: The Coordinating Body transfers the standardised scores from the specialists' and the end-users' polling sheets into the Rating Panel matrix and the Weighting Panel matrix, respectively. Step two: The scores are cross-multiplied to form the standardised Data matrix to derive a ranking on the basis of perceived importance of the planning primers

RATING PANEL
Specialists

PLANNING PRIMERS ~ PPS		Social encounter I	Aesthetic appeal II	Cultural/self-identity III	Functionality IV	Social amenity value V	Privacy VI	Safety VII	Economic opportunity VIII	Recreational options IX	Ecological diversity X
1	Spatial continuity	9	3	90	9	10	1	10	100	7	20
2	Pedestrian density	3	0	6	100	9	0	10	90	6	0
3	Pedestrian streets	0	0	0	0	0	0	0	0	0	0
4	Places to linger	7	45	9	4	3	0	100	0	9	5
5	Sun/wind controls	8	0	0	100	0	0	0	0	0	10
6	Colour/ texture	0	10	5	0	0	0	0	0	90	5
7	Sensory stimuli	2.5	100	9	0	4	0	0	50	6	5
8	Proportions	0	10	7.5	0	2	0	0	0	0	0
9	Human-related scale	95	0	4	0	3	0	100	45	0	0
10	Visual order	0	10	5	3	2	0	10	7.5	2	50
11	Structured space	7.5	70	2	100	5	80	50	75	10	3.5
12	Sense of place	7	100	8	10	50	0	3	9	2	80
13	Cultural identity	90	10	10	3	50	2	2	1	20	0
14	Efficient mobility	9	0	0	100	45	0	10	45	0	0
15	Functionality	100	45	4	10	35	0	90	50	9	0
16	Optimise density	90	0	0	10	7	70	100	90	0	0
17	Building interfaces	0	95	0	9	10	0	75	100	0	0
18	Accessibility	9	0	0	100	80	0	25	75	0	0
19	Personal space	0	100	0	0	0	100	10	0	3	6
20	Neighbourhood scale	90	7.5	3	9	100	25	90	0	0	0
21	Territorial needs	0	10	100	90	4	25	100	3	90	0
22	Pollution-free space	100	0	0	9	10	0	5	0	0	0
23	Presence of others	80	25	0	2	90	0	10	0	0	0
24	Street vending space	7.5	70	0	100	10	0	10	100	0	0
25	Nodes for activity	95	10	3	100	50	0	100	10	0	0
26	Outdoor activities	9	50	7	10	9	0	100	0	10	100
27	Integrate nature	0	90	0	70	100	0	0	0	95	10
28	Biogeography	0	90	0	80	9	0	0	0	2	100
29	Geomorphic impacts	0	0	0	50	4	0	0	0	0	100
30	Benefit-cost ratio	50	90	3	90	8	0	100	10	50	7.5
MEAN		28.95	34.68	9.183	38.93	23.63	10.10	37.00	28.68	13.70	16.73
STANDARD DEVIATION		39.46	38.68	23.2	42.93	31.28	25.49	42.67	37.49	27.69	32.29

UNSTANDARDISED RATING MATRIX

SPATIAL PERFORMANCE GOALS ~ SPGs

Social encounter I	Aesthetic appeal II	Cultural/self-identity III	Functionality IV	Social amenity value V	Privacy VI	Safety VII	Economic opportunity VIII	Recreational options IX	Ecological diversity X
-0.51	-0.82	3.48	-0.70	-0.44	-0.36	-0.63	1.90	-0.24	0.10
-0.66	-0.90	-0.14	1.42	-0.47	-0.40	-0.63	1.64	-0.28	-0.52
-0.73	-0.90	-0.40	-0.91	-0.76	-0.40	-0.87	-0.77	-0.49	-0.52
-0.56	0.27	-0.01	-0.81	-0.66	-0.40	1.48	-0.77	-0.17	-0.36
-0.53	-0.90	-0.40	1.42	-0.76	-0.40	-0.87	-0.77	-0.49	-0.21
-0.73	-0.64	-0.18	-0.91	-0.76	-0.40	-0.87	-0.77	2.76	-0.36
-0.67	1.69	-0.01	-0.91	-0.63	-0.40	-0.87	0.57	-0.28	-0.36
-0.73	-0.64	-0.07	-0.91	-0.69	-0.40	-0.87	-0.77	-0.49	-0.52
1.67	-0.90	-0.22	-0.91	-0.66	-0.40	1.48	0.44	-0.49	-0.52
-0.73	-0.64	-0.18	-0.84	-0.69	-0.40	-0.63	-0.57	-0.42	1.03
-0.54	0.91	-0.31	1.42	-0.60	2.74	0.30	1.24	-0.13	-0.41
-0.56	1.69	-0.05	-0.67	0.84	-0.40	-0.80	-0.53	-0.42	1.96
1.55	-0.64	0.04	-0.84	0.84	-0.32	-0.82	-0.74	0.23	-0.52
-0.51	-0.90	-0.40	1.42	0.68	-0.40	-0.63	0.44	-0.49	-0.52
1.80	0.27	-0.22	-0.67	0.36	-0.40	1.24	0.57	-0.17	-0.52
1.55	-0.90	-0.40	-0.67	-0.53	2.35	1.48	1.64	-0.49	-0.52
-0.73	1.56	-0.40	-0.70	-0.44	-0.40	0.89	1.90	-0.49	-0.52
-0.51	-0.90	-0.40	1.42	1.80	-0.40	-0.28	1.24	-0.49	-0.52
-0.73	1.69	-0.40	-0.91	-0.76	3.53	-0.63	-0.77	-0.39	-0.33
1.55	-0.70	-0.27	-0.70	2.44	0.58	1.24	-0.77	-0.49	-0.52
-0.73	-0.64	3.91	1.19	-0.63	0.58	1.48	-0.69	2.76	-0.52
1.80	-0.90	-0.40	-0.70	-0.44	-0.40	-0.75	-0.77	-0.49	-0.52
1.29	-0.25	-0.40	-0.86	2.12	-0.40	-0.63	-0.77	-0.49	-0.52
-0.54	0.91	-0.40	1.42	-0.44	-0.40	-0.63	1.90	-0.49	-0.52
1.67	-0.64	-0.27	1.42	0.84	-0.40	1.48	-0.50	-0.49	-0.52
-0.51	0.40	-0.09	-0.67	-0.47	-0.40	1.48	-0.77	-0.13	2.58
-0.73	1.43	-0.40	0.72	2.44	-0.40	-0.87	-0.77	2.94	-0.21
-0.73	1.43	-0.40	0.96	-0.47	-0.40	-0.87	-0.77	-0.42	2.58
-0.73	-0.90	-0.40	0.26	-0.63	-0.40	-0.87	-0.77	-0.49	2.58
0.53	1.43	-0.27	1.19	-0.50	-0.40	1.48	-0.50	1.31	-0.29
0.00	0.00	0.00	0.00	0.00	0.00	0.00	0.00	0.00	0.00
1.00	1.00	1.00	1.00	1.00	1.00	1.00	1.00	1.00	1.00

Step one: Coordinating Body transfers the unstandardised scores from the specialists' and the standardised scores from the end-users' polling sheets into the Rating Panel matrix and the Weighting Panel matrix, respectively.

Figure 5.2 Template B: The matrix using unstandardised interval or ratio scores.

For demonstration purposes, Microsoft Excel worksheet software facilitates the mathematical standardisation. The programme offers *fx*, the function wizard, where a sequence of steps is necessary to derive a statistical 'average' or mean, followed by the application of the statistical function. The function in Microsoft Excel software STDEV (or the equivalent) estimates standard deviation based on a sample by returning a normalised value from a distribution characterised by a mean. Thus the standard deviation of the individual unstandardised scores is derived. The Excel worksheet can present a two-row minor matrix for presenting the mean values and standard deviation of each column to assist the process and to provide a running check for consistency.

This procedure is equivalent to applying the equation (Sondheim, 1978):

$$z = (x - \mu) \div \sigma$$

where:

z = value on the (new) standardised scale
x = value on the (old) unstandardised scale
μ = mean value of the unstandardised scores
σ = standard deviation of the unstandardised scores

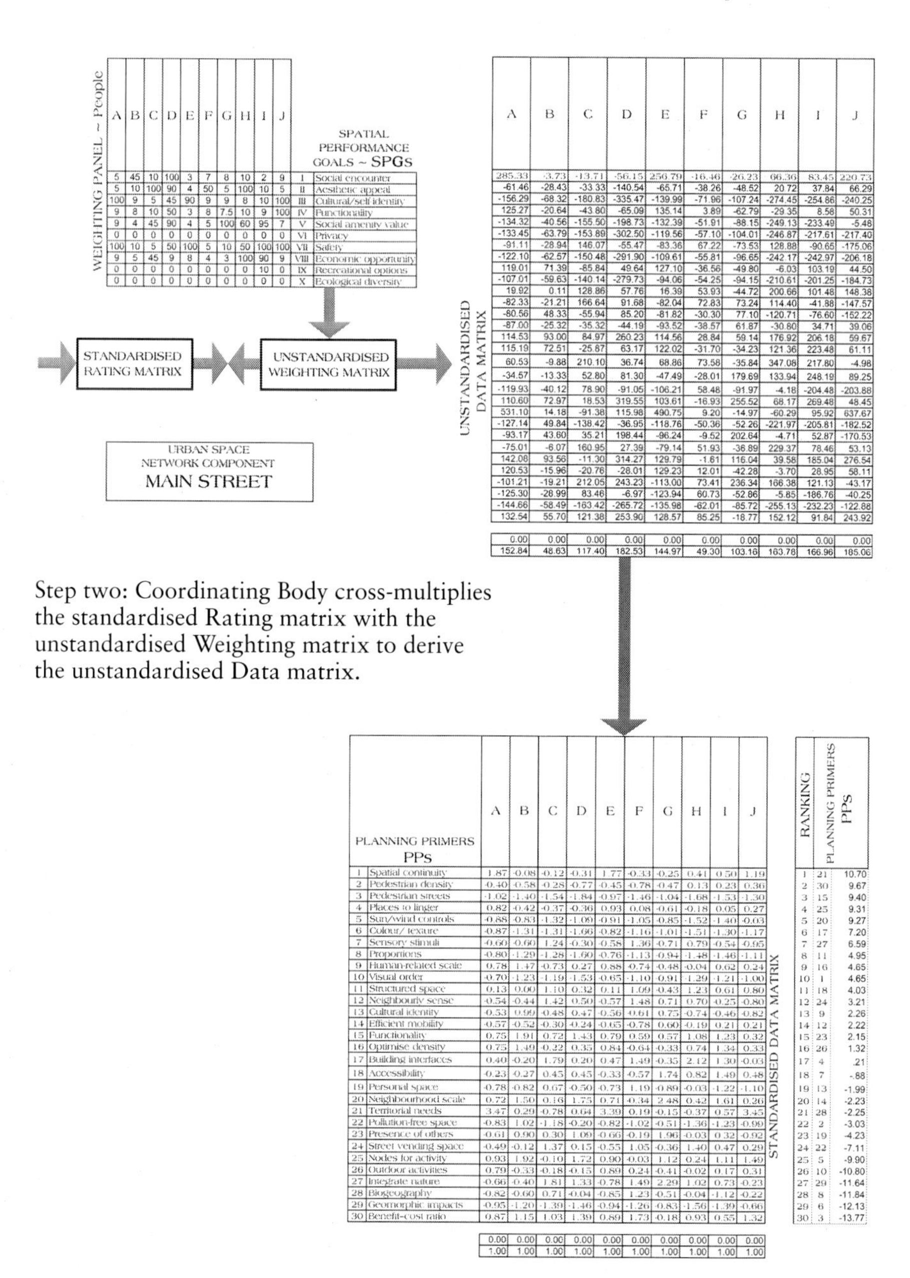

A	B	C	D	E	F	G	H	I	J		SPATIAL PERFORMANCE GOALS ~ SPGs
5	45	10	100	3	7	8	10	2	9	I	Social encounter
5	10	100	90	4	50	5	100	10	5	II	Aesthetic appeal
100	9	5	45	90	9	9	8	10	100	III	Cultural/self identity
9	8	10	50	3	8	7.5	10	9	100	IV	Functionality
9	4	45	90	4	5	100	60	95	7	V	Social amenity value
0	0	0	0	0	0	0	0	0	0	VI	Privacy
100	10	5	50	100	5	10	50	100	100	VII	Safety
9	5	45	9	8	4	3	100	90	9	VIII	Economic opportunity
0	0	0	0	0	0	0	0	10	0	IX	Recreational options
0	0	0	0	0	0	0	0	0	0	X	Ecological diversity

	A	B	C	D	E	F	G	H	I	J
1	285.33	-3.73	-13.71	-56.15	256.79	-16.46	-26.23	66.36	83.45	220.73
2	-61.46	-28.43	-33.33	-140.54	-65.71	-38.26	-48.52	20.72	37.84	66.29
3	-156.29	-68.32	-180.83	-335.47	-139.99	-71.96	-107.24	-274.45	-254.86	-240.25
4	125.27	-20.64	-43.80	-65.09	135.14	3.89	-62.79	-29.35	8.58	50.31
5	-134.32	-40.56	-155.50	-198.73	-132.39	-51.91	-88.15	-249.13	-233.49	-5.48
6	-133.45	-63.79	-153.89	-302.50	-119.56	-57.10	-104.01	-246.87	-217.61	-217.40
7	-91.11	-28.94	146.07	-55.47	-83.36	67.22	-73.53	128.88	-90.65	-175.06
8	-122.10	-62.57	-150.48	-291.90	-109.61	-55.81	-96.65	-242.17	-242.97	-206.18
9	119.01	71.39	-85.84	49.64	127.10	-36.56	-49.80	-6.03	103.19	44.50
10	-107.01	-59.63	-140.14	-279.73	-94.06	-54.25	-94.15	-210.61	-201.25	-184.73
11	19.92	0.11	128.86	57.76	16.39	53.93	-44.72	200.66	101.48	148.38
12	-82.33	-21.21	166.64	91.68	-82.04	72.83	73.24	114.40	-41.88	-147.57
13	-80.56	48.33	-55.94	85.20	-81.82	-30.30	77.10	-120.71	-76.60	-152.22
14	-87.00	-25.32	-35.32	-44.19	-93.52	-38.57	61.87	-30.80	34.71	39.06
15	114.53	93.00	84.97	260.23	114.56	28.84	59.14	176.92	206.18	59.67
16	115.19	72.51	-25.87	63.17	122.02	-31.70	-34.23	121.36	223.48	61.11
17	60.53	-9.88	210.10	36.74	68.86	73.58	-35.84	347.08	217.80	-4.98
18	-34.57	-13.33	52.80	81.30	-47.49	-28.01	179.69	133.94	248.19	89.25
19	-119.93	-40.12	78.90	-91.05	-106.21	58.48	-91.97	-4.18	-204.48	-203.88
20	110.60	72.97	18.53	319.55	103.61	-16.93	255.52	68.17	269.48	48.45
21	531.10	14.18	-91.38	115.98	490.75	9.20	-14.97	-60.29	95.92	637.67
22	-127.14	49.84	-138.42	-36.95	-118.76	-50.36	-52.26	-221.97	-205.81	-182.52
23	-93.17	43.60	35.21	198.44	-96.24	-9.52	202.64	-4.71	52.87	-170.53
24	-75.01	-6.07	160.95	27.39	-79.14	51.93	-36.89	229.37	78.46	53.13
25	142.08	93.56	-11.30	314.27	129.79	-1.61	116.04	39.58	185.04	276.54
26	120.53	-15.96	-20.76	-28.01	129.23	12.01	-42.28	-3.70	28.95	58.11
27	-101.21	-19.21	212.05	243.23	-113.00	73.41	236.34	166.38	121.13	-43.17
28	-125.30	-28.99	83.46	-6.97	-123.94	60.73	-52.86	-5.85	-186.76	-40.25
29	-144.66	-58.49	-163.42	-265.72	-135.98	-62.01	-85.72	-255.13	-232.23	-122.88
30	132.54	55.70	121.38	253.90	128.57	85.25	-18.77	152.12	91.84	243.92
	0.00	0.00	0.00	0.00	0.00	0.00	0.00	0.00	0.00	0.00
	152.84	48.63	117.40	182.53	144.97	49.30	103.16	163.78	166.96	185.06

Step two: Coordinating Body cross-multiplies the standardised Rating matrix with the unstandardised Weighting matrix to derive the unstandardised Data matrix.

	PLANNING PRIMERS PPs	A	B	C	D	E	F	G	H	I	J
1	Spatial continuity	1.87	-0.08	-0.12	-0.31	1.77	-0.33	-0.25	0.41	0.50	1.19
2	Pedestrian density	-0.40	-0.58	-0.28	-0.77	-0.45	-0.78	-0.47	0.13	0.23	0.36
3	Pedestrian streets	-1.02	-1.40	-1.54	-1.84	-0.97	-1.46	-1.04	-1.68	-1.53	-1.30
4	Places to linger	0.82	-0.42	-0.37	-0.36	0.93	0.08	-0.61	-0.18	0.05	0.27
5	Sun/wind controls	-0.88	-0.83	-1.32	-1.09	-0.91	-1.05	-0.85	-1.52	-1.40	-0.03
6	Colour/ texture	-0.87	-1.31	-1.31	-1.66	-0.82	-1.16	-1.01	-1.51	-1.30	-1.17
7	Sensory stimuli	-0.60	-0.60	1.24	-0.30	-0.58	1.36	-0.71	0.79	-0.54	-0.95
8	Proportions	-0.80	-1.29	-1.28	-1.60	-0.76	-1.13	-0.94	-1.48	-1.46	-1.11
9	Human-related scale	0.78	1.47	-0.73	0.27	0.88	-0.74	-0.48	-0.04	0.62	0.24
10	Visual order	-0.70	-1.23	-1.19	-1.53	-0.65	-1.10	-0.91	-1.29	-1.21	-1.00
11	Structured space	0.13	0.00	1.10	0.32	0.11	1.09	-0.43	1.23	0.61	0.80
12	Neighbourly sense	-0.54	-0.44	1.42	0.50	-0.57	1.48	0.71	0.70	-0.25	-0.80
13	Cultural identity	-0.53	0.99	-0.48	0.47	-0.56	-0.61	0.75	-0.74	-0.46	-0.82
14	Efficient mobility	-0.57	-0.52	-0.30	-0.24	-0.65	-0.78	0.60	-0.19	0.21	0.21
15	Functionality	0.75	1.91	0.72	1.43	0.79	0.59	0.57	1.08	1.23	0.32
16	Optimise density	0.75	1.49	-0.22	0.35	0.84	-0.64	-0.33	0.74	1.34	0.33
17	Building interfaces	0.40	-0.20	1.79	0.20	0.47	1.49	-0.35	2.12	1.30	-0.03
18	Accessibility	-0.23	-0.27	0.45	0.45	-0.33	-0.57	1.74	0.82	1.49	0.48
19	Personal space	-0.78	-0.82	0.67	-0.50	-0.73	1.19	-0.89	-0.03	-1.22	-1.10
20	Neighbourhood scale	0.72	1.50	0.16	1.75	0.71	-0.34	2.48	0.42	1.61	0.26
21	Territorial needs	3.47	0.29	-0.78	0.64	3.39	0.19	-0.15	-0.37	0.57	3.45
22	Pollution-free space	-0.83	1.02	-1.18	-0.20	-0.82	-1.02	-0.51	-1.36	-1.23	-0.99
23	Presence of others	-0.61	0.90	0.30	1.09	-0.66	-0.19	1.96	-0.03	0.32	-0.92
24	Street vending space	-0.49	-0.12	1.37	0.15	-0.55	1.05	-0.36	1.40	0.47	0.29
25	Nodes for activity	0.93	1.92	-0.10	1.72	0.90	-0.03	1.12	0.24	1.11	1.49
26	Outdoor activities	0.79	-0.33	-0.18	-0.15	0.89	0.24	-0.41	-0.02	0.17	0.31
27	Integrate nature	-0.66	-0.40	1.81	1.33	-0.78	1.49	2.29	1.02	0.73	-0.23
28	Biogeography	-0.82	-0.60	0.71	-0.04	-0.85	1.23	-0.51	-0.04	-1.12	-0.22
29	Geomorphic impacts	-0.95	-1.20	-1.39	-1.46	-0.94	-1.26	-0.83	-1.56	-1.39	-0.66
30	Benefit-cost ratio	0.87	1.15	1.03	1.39	0.89	1.73	-0.18	0.93	0.55	1.32
		0.00	0.00	0.00	0.00	0.00	0.00	0.00	0.00	0.00	0.00
		1.00	1.00	1.00	1.00	1.00	1.00	1.00	1.00	1.00	1.00

RANKING	PLANNING PRIMERS	PPs
1	21	10.70
2	30	9.67
3	15	9.40
4	25	9.31
5	20	9.27
6	17	7.20
7	27	6.59
8	11	4.95
9	16	4.65
10	1	4.65
11	18	4.03
12	24	3.21
13	9	2.26
14	12	2.22
15	23	2.15
16	26	1.32
17	4	.21
18	7	-.88
19	13	-1.99
20	14	-2.23
21	28	-2.25
22	2	-3.03
23	19	-4.23
24	22	-7.11
25	5	-9.90
26	10	-10.80
27	29	-11.64
28	8	-11.84
29	6	-12.13
30	3	-13.77

Step three: The unstandardised scores in the Data matrix are standardised to derive a ranking for the planning primers by perceived importance.

This equation ensures that the mean of each scheme will be zero and thus that each scheme will be weighted identically.

Operationalising the unstandardised procedure in a hypothetical situation

To facilitate a reliable outcome, handout Polling Sheets 1 and 2 (Appendices 1 and 2) could be prepared for both the Weighting and the Rating Panels and a cognitive map of the particular urban spatial component under consideration to provide site-specific reference. The two sets of panellists are simply required to fill in their evaluations in the spaces provided on the Polling Sheets. Weighting scores by the community are focused on the distillation of their perceived socio-cultural needs that are transposed as SPGs. Rating scores by the specialists on the Rating Panel would be based on the realisation of the SPGs in relation to the listed PPs.These would then be transferred to the matrices by the Coordinating Body.

Once rating scores have been standardised using the *fx* function, cross-multiplication follows of the standardised Rating matrix with the unstandardised Weighting matrix to produce the unstandardised Data matrix. Returning to *fx*, the function wizard, standardised Data matrix is achieved, which in effect provides the ranking of importance for PPs in the attainment of the listed SPGs. The ranking of the PPs is the outcome of the perceived importance of the listed SPGs transposed into specific PPs. In the next stage, planning actions can be determined from the latter. Due to actual end-user involvement as well as specialist participation, the hierarchical evaluation of priorities with respect to a particular urban space project can be considered as having been democratically derived and thus provides a more culture-driven planning base. As a potential design and planning tool, the methodological outcome equips the specialist where dependence on training, creative insight and experience will take the project further.

With the vast field of research to back urban design and planning fields, the source material presented in Chapter Seven is included as a ready reference or checklist for the shapers and designers of urban space.

References

Sondheim, M.W. "A Comprehensive Methodology for Assessing Environmental Impact." *Journal of Environmental Management* 6 (1978): 27–42.

UN-Habitat for a Better Urban Future. "Visioning as a Participatory Planning Tool" (2012). Available at: http://led.co.za/sites/default/files/cabinet/orgname-raw/document/2012/better_cities_for_all.pdf, accessed 15 June 2015.

Chapter Six

The making of 'place'

For all urban development, the starting point should be a holistic assessment of the processes whereby the goals are to be achieved. Left to the ordinary urban dweller, a more organically ordered social space is generally the result; however, specialisation in the urban design and architectural spheres has tended to fragment the expertise, resulting in a potential loss of those human qualities that enable a better life under urban conditions. Taken to an extreme, failure to meet the cultural needs of the community, the urban dweller, the end-user could threaten cognitive perceptions of the social environment, potentially with sociological consequences.

Broadly defined design routes are the pragmatic, the iconic, the analogical and the canonic. Pragmatic design employs available resources to establish building form; iconic is the literal repetition of tried and tested form, such as the Greek temple epitomised by the columned portico; analogical defines the transfer of ideas from one context to another; and canonic involves the use of a geometric grid or a proportional system. Although seemingly mutually exclusive, as expressed in their pure form, the soft edges of these design routes make overlap probable rather than presenting a ready definition.

> *Place: particular part of space occupied by a person or thing, city, town, village etc.; residence, dwelling; small group of houses round a square etc.; country house with surroundings; building or area devoted to specified purpose (place of amusement).*
>
> (*South African Pocket Oxford Dictionary*, 1987: 575)

The cultural dimension

Stylistic expression in both architecture and urban design can be shown to be directly related to cultural preference. Some theories suggest an innate affinity in cultures to express uniform design language which can be borne out by example. Typically, the design criteria of urban social space should meet the cultural needs of communities in different ways. In the post-millennium era, the amenity value of the social environment will decline unless the cultural preferences of the end-user are satisfied.

Cultural proclivity, or natural inclination, a behavioural phenomenon that spreads from person to person within a culture, became the focus of a field of study called 'memetics' which arose in the 1990s. The concepts and transmission of 'memes' in terms of an evolutionary model were explored. Transmitted from one mind to another, some researchers regard memes as analogous to genes, self-replicating and responding to environmental influences. Richard Dawkins coined the term 'meme' – which derives from the Greek word *mimema* (something imitated) – in 1976 (Dawkins, 2006). The relevance of this study is that it resonates with the cultural trends in communities, even nations, in many fields, including art, design, music, philosophy, writing, fashion and lifestyle. Dawkins likens the process by which memes survive and change through the evolution of culture to the natural selection of genes in biological evolution.

In *Cultural Software: A Theory of Ideology*, Balkin (1994) maintains that memes form narratives, networks of cultural associations and a variety of different mental structures. This is an interesting philosophy with which to begin understanding how the dynamics of culture are expressed in the living environment, and by association in architectural style and the ordering of public space. The collective mindset is evident in all indigenous cultures down the ages: the timeless vocabularies of design and style such as Classicism or Gothic in Europe, or the vernacular styles of Russia, the Middle East, Africa and China, to name only a few. The medina cities in Morocco remain places of vibrant Moroccan culture, essentially large open spaces surrounded by vending in the open or in arcades, enabling social intercourse and trade.

Writing about architecture, Sudjic (2006: 9) holds that

> There may be no fixed political meaning to a given architectural language, but that does not mean that architecture lacks the potential to assume a political aspect . . . Few successful architects can avoid producing buildings with a political dimension at some point in their career, whether they want to or not. And almost all political leaders find themselves using architects for political purposes.

Similarly, urban social space can potentially become a political statement rather than the outcome of a democratic process.

Design legacies can also be evaluated for their response to the expediencies of the times, and to the needs of a diversity of end-users. In the once-colonised countries of Africa, which experienced imported cultural values and shared symbiotic relationships with political systems and the prevailing economies, the withdrawal of colonial assuredness left behind naivety that afforded no effective counter to a 'free-for-all' mindset. On the other hand, liberation, or empowerment, can spawn an unstoppable creative drive evident in the Africanisation of cities, the products of colonial influence, such as in Johannesburg in South Africa – the African Renaissance at work, given impetus through the right to decide.

In the past, in the developed world, forms of mobility were in scale with the established infrastructural legacies of older cities, and people moved on foot, on bicycle or on the public omnibus. Today the economically empowered masses aspire towards private motor-car ownership, meaning that the cultural lifestyle and the world view of the average person have shifted into a higher gear, in terms of both travel time and the impact of scale on existing movement systems. This rapid rise of private vehicle ownership in emerging markets and developing countries has important implications for transport and environmental policies, as well as for how urban space is allocated to resolve disparate spatial demands. It is likely that this growth in the use of the private motor car, and thus in the physical space required for roads and infrastructure within the urban environment, will be met by instant action unless the urban dweller places demands on those who determine policy. Cultural landscapes are no longer confined to the exclusive use of local communities.

Coupled with the growth in private car ownership is the expansion in world travel. Where the nearest seaside resort once would have been the choice for the annual holiday, affluence, particularly in the developed world, has enabled the rise of the giant global tourism industry. The economies of whole nations benefit from seasonal economic injections from the touring masses. In turn, cities have become brand destinations for packaged tours, and the original populations of remote villages have been replaced by the seasonal influx of the city dweller. In the process the regional vernacular has yielded to sophisticated typologies and variations.

For the future, an unanswered question remains: what role should those who shape our living environments play in response to today's global issues? Urban designers still tend to be in the rearguard of commitment to the pressing post-millennium issues. The global economic meltdown provides a strong case for those who design the urban space to embrace the new challenges. In the urban environment, for example, the failure to meet the cultural needs of the community – the end user – threatens the amenity value of the social environment with potentially significant sociological consequences.

For an urban designer or planner, the task can be likened to a journey with various possible routes along which design goals might be satisfied. Success lies in choosing the right route. The detachment of planners and urban designers from the social needs of communities is epitomised in the poor performance of many urban environments. At best, the dismissal of the real needs of the users of the urban environment can be described as prescriptive; at worst, it might be seen as a crime of social dimensions.

Adopting the line that a response to culture-specific expectations should be an important factor in planning policy raises another issue – human rights. Ironically, urban dwellers' participation in the shaping of their own habitats is a sphere of human rights that has not yet enjoyed much political accountability. The right to a better environment is germane to greater productivity and development of each individual's potential and that of the community as a whole. Where millions in urban situations are forced to live in close proximity and encounter a form of rivalry for their own space, the cultural expectations of the urban dweller regarding the need for privacy, self-fulfilment, identity, bonding of communities, work options and recreational opportunity have not been given the attention they deserve.

Cultural expectations are a well-researched field and most evidence points to them being cross-cultural and universally unvarying. Starting with the end-user is obviously an imperative.

Considering historical precedents, it is most often in the sphere of residential development or redevelopment that reshapers of the urban environment are afforded the opportunity to restore urban environments to vitality and productiveness. Housing is directly associated with the round-the-clock needs of the individual and the community, and perhaps it provides the strongest potential for catalytic change or for urban renewal. It is significant that goals for sustainable neighbourhoods and even cities can often be achieved through new large-scale housing projects.

Conservation ethos

The idea of 'sustainable development' is central to many debates about future economic progress, from local to global, and definitions of the concept abound. Yet in all the literature there is a common thread which identifies it as a system devised for ensuring that social and environmental goals are sustained through prudent human and natural resource management, while providing for short- and long-term economic horizons. Sustainability through good stewardship of the earth's resources will provide for the needs of the least advantaged in today's society (intragenerational equity) and ensure fairness for future generations (intergenerational equity).

Aiming to fill the information gap, and perhaps to provide better understanding of the complexity of the issue, various commentators have attempted to identify the pivotal issues that constitute sustainability.

Externalities are often conveniently overlooked by the developer and usually not granted significance by the approval authority. The natural environment should not be viewed in isolation, but seen in context with social and cultural issues that are potentially real yet go unaddressed where the impacts, either positive or negative, are difficult to compute.

In all countries the state also has a role to play in promoting sustainable development, for example through granting tax credits as incentives for environmentally correct deployment of public funds. In the first year of the new millennium, New York State introduced a pioneering scheme offering tax credits with supporting legislation to encourage 'green' design in one of the world's densest urban environments.

The designer and the patron developer are equally accountable for transforming the environment through development projects that inevitably will disturb the established biological diversity.

Urban morphology

From an urban planning and design perspective, a transportation framework will characterise the basic morphology of a city. In new situations a pattern of hierarchical transportation routes will be key to the structuring and growth of the urban environment as well as the potential for 'capacity' development.

Depending on the type of mobility, such as by motor vehicle or bicycle or on foot, it is important that a movement system does not destroy the integrity of the public space with which it links and through which it passes. Proper planning can employ devices to avoid the bisection of a space; alternatively, a movement system could pass through axially, obliquely or along the periphery of a space. A movement system can also be planned to exploit three-dimensional topography where changes in urban levels can enhance the urban spatial character. Italian medieval towns, such as Assisi and Lucca, or the famous Piazza di Spagna in Rome, are outstanding examples of the power of level changes to preserve the visual qualities and amenity value of urban space.

The movement system can become the means towards more efficient land usage through which wider urban functions may be served. In historical or existing urban agglomerations, this form of urban structuring will mostly be a given, in either an imposed or a more dynamic configuration. Movement patterns within an urban environment are broadly represented by the following typical configurations, in either pure or composite form:

- Linear configurations that are a primary organising element catering for cars, bicycles, people and services. As part of a movement system, they are not confined to a straight line, but could be slow or tight curvilinear. They could also be segmented, depending on whether they are planned strictly for cars or for people.
- Grid systems create nodes at regular intersections that yield square or rectangular fields of space. A useful city case study of the influence of topography on the grid configuration of streets is San Francisco, where the public transport system exploits the characteristics of a difficult terrain to striking advantage. The needs of the city have exploited the attributes of the topography and produced an energy-efficient transport system.
- Network configuration that is in essence a random system connecting specific important nodal points in urban space.

- Radial systems that are capable of providing efficient circulation, providing they are supplemented by concentric circulation and depending on other factors, including topography.
- Spiral configurations that are continuous systems originating from a central point and becoming increasingly distant from it. Unless planned to create a specific spatial experience, the choice of such a system would probably be dictated by topography. Italian hillside towns provide good precedents for spiral corridor systems.
- Composite configurations that are more common than the preceding pure forms, and the movement systems of most towns that have evolved organically from dynamic growth transposed through socially and economically determined desire lines. The resultant richness of spatial diversity at the intersections of a composite configuration can be well exploited for social and economic vitality.

Kayvan Karimi discusses space syntax, concluding that the approach proposed has to be spatial "since urban design is about shaping spaces for the people and society." The question of scales has to be dealt with: "An urban system manifests itself in many scales: an urban room, a public space, a neighbourhood, a district, an entire city and even a region." Furthermore, given the complexity of synthesising the multifaceted aspect of urban design and planning, the conclusion is that it is "quite apparent why the use of analytical methods in urban design has been fairly restricted: it is not very easy to find a methodology that could fulfil all these criteria."

(Karimi, 2012: 304)

Density criteria

Density is generally defined as the ratio between the population of a given area and the area itself. Either gross density or net density may be calculated, with the latter referring to the ratio of population to *residential* land (with land set aside for other uses not included in the calculation).

Density is often the most commonly accepted indicator as a reference for the amount of land needed to support facilities with regard to a given population and it is also an indicator of the type of physical development. This inevitably varies with the circumstances of the layout being planned. For example, site topography could relieve the perception of 'denseness', as can be seen on hilly terrain, as in the case of Jerusalem, Barcelona and Athens. When translated into simple graphics, Caminos and Goethert's (1978) Land Utilization Index (LUI; see below) allows quick visual comparisons among several layout alternatives. This method enables planners to conduct initial studies with a view to optimising densities, so that land use efficiency becomes clearer at an earlier stage without the need for heavy expenditure in terms of finance or time.

Whatever methodology is adopted to determine optimum density, an understanding of how the socio-cultural needs of urban communities transform into identifiable physical patterns is seminal to good urban planning: people-inspired historical settlements should be inspirational for planners. Apart from the potential for effecting land-use efficiency, the starting point for formal planning is acceptance of the phenomenon of the social need/spatial form interdependency.

The potential catalyst

Replacing blighted or downgraded sites becomes possible, for example, when a city hosts the Olympic Games or another mega-sports event where significant numbers of participants must be housed. Three scenarios for housing development could shape urban renewal:

- Where residential districts take the form of 'urban redevelopment', buildings in need of renovation would supplement new development and make use of the existing amenity infrastructure and urban landscaping. This would involve retaining parts of the old and merging them with the new into an upgraded fabric, such as for the Olympic Games in Barcelona, 1992. Redevelopment work generally takes the form of an implant into the existing urban structural and social situations, or development of a 'brownfield' site within a metropolitan area. The knock-on effect on neighbouring districts and vice versa, however, should be considered as such interventions may spark revitalisation of peripheral areas as well or, equally, may cause their rapid degeneration into slums. An effective social programme to deal with residents' negative perceptions of the redevelopment site and surrounding areas should form part of any redevelopment strategy.
- Where residential districts take the form of 'urban expansion', expediency sometimes favours the use of 'greenfield' sites on the outskirts of town, where controls are not as rigidly entrenched and rapid preparation and completion of housing and urban space projects can be achieved to reduce development costs. The downside is that such development is often characterised by physical isolation, functionally separating the town's living areas from workplaces. Rapid transportation modes become imperative, although invariably the construction and upgrading of transportation routes lags behind such development, thus creating social and economic hardship for the newly housed communities.
- Where residential districts take the form of 'new urban building', in general such development can be characterised by the 'new town' concept, notably in England and Israel. In England such development

> has been due primarily to the pressure of population numbers, or the desire to locate people closer to employment opportunities. In Israel the new towns represent specific settlement measures for opening up undeveloped areas, such as the desert, and for settling people from a diversity of cultures in the Jewish Diaspora. In this concept the basic planning conditions can be self-imposed, and they offer scope for 'ideal planning' with central town amenities, jobs, recreation areas and residential districts appearing simultaneously.

The above new development interventions are primarily aimed at providing for residential community life, but they represent a potentially effective starting point for upgrading jaded city environments and the chance to focus on urban social spaces. Utilising these scenarios, urban designers and planners would be able to use their creative energies to address environmental concerns with a renewed sense of social responsibility, linked with their commitment to planning for productive urban living.

Sense of neighbourhood

In recent times various individuals and government agencies have expressed interest in learning more from the past experiences and achievements of man as builder of his own environment and about the preservation and restoration of historic/traditional architecture.

Perceptions play a significant part in fostering a sense of belonging in an ideal neighbourhood, and optimum population threshold is an important factor in effective social networking and bonding. The available evidence suggests that:

- people identify with neighbourhoods that have extremely small populations;
- such neighbourhoods are small in area; and
- a major road through a neighbourhood destroys the potential for bonding.

The Western experience is that, if a population is over 1500 people, such a group finds it difficult to coordinate itself to reach decisions about important issues affecting its common interests. Some sociologists set the figure even lower – at 500 people.

Research in the United States concludes that the optimum physical area for a sense of neighbourhood is between one and three blocks. A more significant factor, however, is that a "neighbourhood can only have a strong identity if it is protected from heavy traffic" (Alexander *et al.*, 1977: 82). In their chapter on the 'identifiable neighbourhood', Alexander *et al.* advocate that neighbourhoods should not be more than 300 metres across, with a population of no more than 400–500 people, and major roads must be kept out.

According to the Prophet Mohammed, each person in a community should take care of seven neighbours around himself. This is Islam's basic concept of community and neighbourhood (*mohalia*), and the basis for all Muslim settlement formations (Talib, 1984).

The following principles (Morkel, 1988) should be observed with prototypical small plot layouts:

- The plot, which is generally narrow on its street frontage and deep in its extent back from the street, reduces the length of the service infrastructure along the street frontage corresponding to each plot. Financial and land resources for other capital works would thereby be liberated for amenity purposes.
- The road system should be designed to minimise through traffic in residential areas, thereby allowing for a large reduction in the width of local-access residential streets. Similarly, this would lead to a reduction in the amount of land and road infrastructure corresponding to each plot.
- The house should be placed close to the street to conserve the unbuilt-on area of the plot as a single area for private use, rather than a series of fragmented and unusable side-spaces. The house extending across the full width of the street frontage will provide a secure, private area to the rear of the site. In this way, the narrower frontage on to the public environment is reduced and maintenance is minimised.
- Extensions to the rear of the house should be kept to the perimeter of the plot to ensure that the area of the private social space is maximised.
- Panhandle sites become possible with consequent efficiency in the layout of the service infrastructure.

When a building fronts directly on to public spaces, it is advantageous that "the public edge of the building should house activities which benefit from interaction with the public realm, and can contribute to the life of the public space itself" (Bentley *et al.*, 1985: 63–64). To achieve this:

- Locate as many entrances as possible in such positions that comings and goings are directly visible from the public space.
- Encourage compatible uses within the buildings to spill out into the public area. This principle applies to uses on the ground and first floors.
- Even if there are no public uses, most buildings contain activities which can contribute to the animation of the public space itself.
- It is still necessary to preserve the privacy of the indoor activity, so that the users will not feel the need to screen themselves totally from the public space. This privacy can be achieved by horizontal distance, a change in level or both.
- The usefulness of the building edge is important for people-watching and is greatly increased by the provision of places to sit.

With the development of all settlements there are thresholds of tolerance regarding density. Although not exhaustive, as a rule of thumb, the test criteria conceived by Caminos and Goethert (1978) could be used as a guide.

Clusters and common land

In a survey of 150 people in Levittown, New York, it was found that all of them were engaged in some pattern of regular visiting with their neighbours (Gans, 1991). This visiting pattern is significant in that it underlines the fact that people want be part of a neighbourhood cluster. The extent to which the opportunity to visit is conducted formally or informally in a neighbourhood would depend on cultural and socio-economic factors. On a typical block each home is at the centre of its own cluster, demonstrating that the social patterning continues even when the conventional block layout, or neighbourhood plan, is not specifically planned as cluster units and instead tends to promote anonymity.

To replace a grid-like array of houses on a street, clustering of a more personal nature gives people immediate and effective control over their common land. "A cluster is a dynamic social structure, which takes physical shape, and is governed above all by the common land at its heart and by the fluidity of the relations between the individual families and this common land" (Alexander *et al.*, 1977: 198). Control over the common space reinforces the community and is wholly important to successful residential neighbourhoods. Further, Alexander *et al.* (1977: 198) state that "the cluster of land and homes immediately around one's own home is of special importance . . . and it is the natural focus of neighbourly interaction."

The urge to cluster emerges in the presence of certain supporting factors. On the basis of a community keeping in touch and meeting internally for decision-making, Alexander *et al.* (1985) observe the following pattern:

- the clusters seem to work best if they each comprise eight to twelve houses;
- more than twelve houses and the balance is strained;
- in all cases common land which is shared by the cluster is an essential ingredient; and
- ownership is essential for the clustering pattern to take hold, and shared ownership of the social space reinforces the common interest.

Alexander *et al.* (1977) recommend that houses should therefore be arranged in broadly identifiable clusters of eight to twelve households around some common land and paths. Clusters should also be arranged so that *anyone* can walk through them without feeling like a trespasser.

In residential contexts, clustering is observed throughout history where there has been no regimentation through formal planning. It is a spontaneous process that Rapoport (1977: 249) states: "tends to occur in cities based on perceived homogeneity, differing interpretations of environmental quality, lifestyles, symbol systems, and defences against overload and stress." Clustering in dense conurbations enables mutual help, assimilation of new incomers, and the urbanisation and preservation of certain institutions. It also helps to maintain familiar controls and cultural patterns. It is conceivable that "people who are already under great stress need the support of familiar and even 'prosthetic' environments, as groups who have lowered competence, or are in a state of cultural docility, are more vulnerable" (Rapoport, 1977: 259). In Africa there is a long tradition of identifying territory with ethnic groups. In more recent examples, clustering patterns are also observable in squatter settlements.

Other urban commentators have shown that in dense city environments a division into quite distinct and separate areas on the bases of place of origin, age, occupation, home-ownership, recency of arrival and tribal origin is discernible. A common feature in most modern town planning practice is the inclusion of a main gate in a housing precinct in order to heighten the distinctiveness of the area and give it a unique identity.

> *"People will not feel comfortable in their houses unless a group of houses forms a cluster, with the public land between them jointly owned by all the householders" and "every boundary in the city which has important human meaning – the boundary of a building cluster, a neighbourhood, a precinct – [should be marked by] great gateways where the major entering paths cross the boundary."*
>
> (Alexander *et al.*, 1977: 198, 278)

Furthermore, common land should be provided as a social necessity: first, to "make it possible for people to feel comfortable outside their buildings and their private territory"; and, second, because "common land acts as a meeting place for people" (Alexander *et al.*, 1985: 339). There should be enough common land to be useful and to accommodate children's games and small gatherings. Alexander *et al.* (1985: 339) suggest that "the amount of common land needed in a neighbourhood is in the order of twenty-five per cent of the land held privately." Motor vehicles should on no account be allowed to dominate this land.

> *Outlining the role and value of public space has long been a subject of academic, political, and professional debate. At the most basic level public space can be defined as publicly owned land that, in theory, is open and accessible to all members of a given community – regardless of gender, race, ethnicity, age, or socio-economic level.*
>
> *Access to adequate public space and basic services is an essential human right, and ensuring the availability of these resources in developing and newly urbanizing countries where they are lacking is of paramount importance.*
>
> (MacKenzie, n.d.)

Spatial closure and visual order

Streets that are visually enclosed tend to avoid the impression of being thoroughfares, and provide better settings for social interaction. It is not only the public squares of old towns that merit study but also the configuration of their streets. The spatial enclosure they achieve is equally important to good urban design. Sitte (1965: 61) states that "The ideal street must form a completely enclosed unit. The more one's impressions are confined within it, the more perfect will be its tableau: one feels at ease in a space where the gaze cannot be lost in infinity."

Straight roads are necessary today and they are often very imposing. Sitte condemns their mechanical employment, *a priori*, without concern for the configuration of the terrain or other local circumstances. He states (Sitte, 1965: 67):

> If the meandering line is more picturesque, the straight one is more monumental; but we cannot subsist from monumentality alone, and it would be desirable that the builders of modern cities do not abuse the one or the other, but make use of them both as appropriate, in order to give to each district which they lay out an aspect in conformity with its purpose.

Principles of visual order that allow diversity without monotony and provide spatial character and integrity are useful goals in the design of city spaces. Such 'ordering principles' as axial, symmetrical, hierarchical, rhythmic/repetitive, transformative and the use of a 'datum' line device can present the beholder with subliminal evidence of an underlying visual ordering.

The application of principles for designing 'ordered' urban space can be synthesised as follows (Ching, 1979: 292):

- An axis can be established by a symmetrical or asymmetrical arrangement of forms and spaces.
- There are two types of symmetry: bilateral symmetry, which is the balanced arrangement of two equivalent elements about a common axis, and radial symmetry, which consists of equivalent elements balanced about two or more axes that intersect at a central point.
- A form or space can be made significant by being made visibly unique, by endowing the shape with exceptional size, shape or location or a composite form of these principles.
- Rhythm employs the fundamental principle of repetition, of which the simplest form is linear. Alternatives include grouping of elements by size, shape or detail.
- Transformation allows the systematic manipulation of a typical, appropriate, architectural model, geometric form or shape through a discreet evolution to respond to the specific context of the design at hand.

- A datum is a device in the form of a line, plane or volume that has the property of organising a random pattern of elements through its regularity, continuity and constant presence. As a device, a datum must have sufficient scale to perform its function effectively.

The relaxed concepts of Sitte (1965) and the geometric principles identified by Ching (1979) are not mutually exclusive, but rather provide the urban designer with a set of time-tested conventions for developing a well-conceived urban spatial canvas for architecture.

Respect for the site

Land characteristics are situation specific, as are natural attributes. The manner in which a programme is set up to transform a site and manage building operations is demonstrably the first measure of resource-mindedness. Traditional methods using human labour to prepare a site for building or landscaping have been replaced by massive time- and labour-saving earth-moving technology and explosive devices. Rather than permit the site to inform the design, commonly used modern mechanised methods have the capacity to alter the characteristics of the site within hours to suit the design. In the process of remodelling the site, respect for it in terms of its intrinsic characteristics, particularly in the case of a 'greenfield' site, is bypassed. Wilfully ignoring the physical and the resource attributes of a site removes its 'sense of place' – a process of energy-spent destruction that incurs significant environmental cost. The habitats of species and culturally important sites in the wider context could, by extension, be demeaned by the radical transformation of a new adjoining site.

An informed understanding of potential impacts should be dealt with on a methodical basis. It is therefore more constructive at the commencement of a project to develop a checklist rather than a 'green scorecard'. By defining environmental issues from the outset, potential impacts should not fall through the net.

A methodological approach utilising, for example, the matrix procedure developed by Dr Luna Leopold and colleagues in 1971 could be useful for a preliminary impact assessment. Developing two data sets – one related to environmental elements and the other to project actions – as the coordinates of a matrix, it is possible to expand the scope and usefulness of a checklist. Crossed with a diagonal line, each cell is able to receive two numerical or colour-coded scores: first the magnitude and then the importance of the impact. By considering each of the envisaged project actions in the context of each site-specific environmental element, and by marking each cell of the matrix above (magnitude) and below (importance) a diagonal line, the completed matrix simulates a near-graphic depiction through numbers, symbols or shadings of all cells with above-average impacts and their importance. The matrix could be expanded to include ratings for risk or uncertainty (Fuggle and Rabie, 1983: 768).

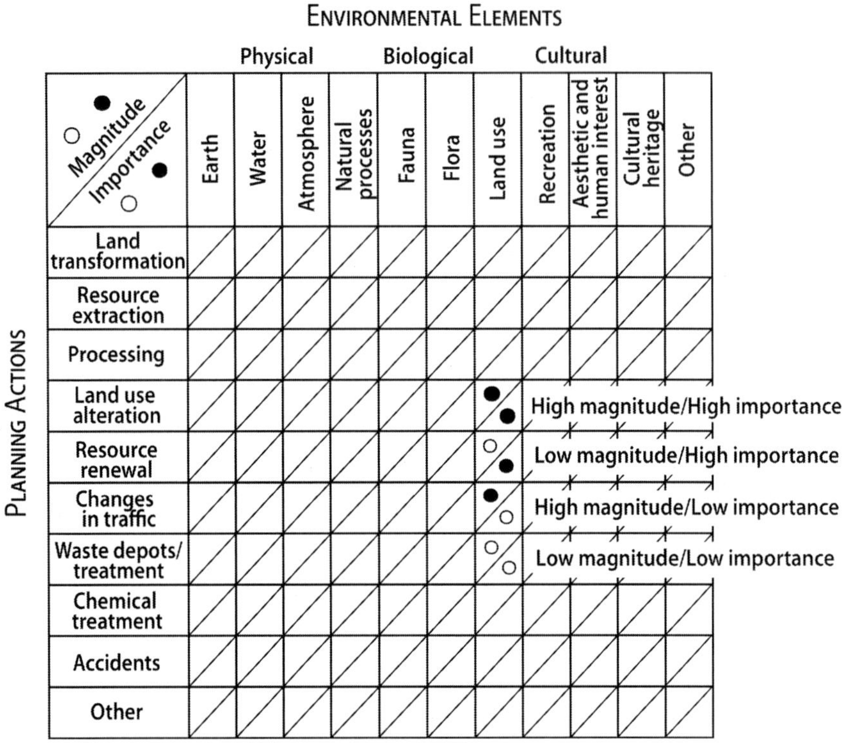

ENVIRONMENTAL ELEMENTS

PLANNING ACTIONS (Magnitude ● ○ / Importance ● ○)	Physical: Earth	Water	Atmosphere	Natural processes	Biological: Fauna	Flora	Land use	Cultural: Recreation	Aesthetic and human interest	Cultural heritage	Other
Land transformation											
Resource extraction											
Processing											
Land use alteration							● ●	High magnitude/High importance			
Resource renewal							○ ●	Low magnitude/High importance			
Changes in traffic							● ○	High magnitude/Low importance			
Waste depots/ treatment							○ ○	Low magnitude/Low importance			
Chemical treatment											
Accidents											
Other											

Figure 6.1 Environmental scoping matrix

Utilising such tools as an initial scoping framework in the conduct of their practices, urban designers and planners could be afforded the basic means to become environmental generalists. A preliminary checklist at the outset of a project would at least determine whether further specialist expertise is needed to complete a thorough investigation based on potential impacts that have been identified. By using this initial step to precede proper environmental impact assessments, appropriate mitigating measures may be developed for a project. In this way practitioners shaping the environment can contribute towards the protection of the biosphere with equanimity while satisfying the development goals of their clients.

Working with climate

Together with a site's geophysical and ecological characteristics, climate, viewed in the overall perspective of human settlement, is the single most important seasonal constant in our landscape. Socio-economic and political conditions, style preferences and aesthetic sensibility will evolve, but climate remains on a discernible cyclical course. Historical studies of settlement show that even the ancient civilisations recognised regional climatic adaptation as an essential principle in the creation of the human habitat.

Harnessing the potential offered by the climate can assert a dramatic effect on a design and make a profound difference to its energy and water demands. Climatically responsive open space can enhance the urban dweller's sense of wellbeing while enabling them to experience the external climate of the place – the diurnal and seasonal changes. In so doing, the blandness of spending long working hours indoors in an otherwise artificial environment, invariably controlled throughout the year, can be relieved.

An important factor in climate-conscious design is the position and angle of the solar arc in both winter and summer. Armed with data on seasonal solar penetration, the optimum orientation of the amenities of urban social spaces and the details of the design can be determined. Solar charts to refine orientation and solar control elements should be seen as indispensable design aids for the urban designer and planner.

It is useful to compare graphically the variations in solar radiation intensity on horizontal and vertical surfaces for different orientations. The following observations emerge for two contrasting locations, one at the equator and the other at 33 degrees south of the equator:

- In both locations, especially at the equator, the horizontal surface receives the greater intensity.
- East- and west-facing walls receive high intensities in the equatorial location and similarly at the higher latitude.
- In the equatorial location, north and south walls receive the least intensity and only for short periods of the year.
- At the high southern latitude, the north-facing wall receives the highest intensity in winter, when the sun's arc is lower, but very little in the summer.

At some latitudes, solar heat gain on the west side can be particularly troublesome as its maximum intensity coincides with the hottest part of the day. The proviso is that these conditions are valid in situations where all other factors are equal (Koenigsberger *et al.*, 1974).

Taking three contrasting climate types – the Mediterranean climate with winter rainfall, a distinctly hot and dry but minimal summer rainfall region, and a hot and humid region – differing approaches would be required towards the layout and orientation of entire developments. Mediterranean climates are usually coastal, with hot and dry summers and cooler nights. Winters, with high rainfall, are cold but milder than those of inland regions, while coastal winds predominate in the summer.

Layout and design of buildings would favour:

- urban layouts such as traditionally compact, to provide protection for external spaces from coastal winds;

- the longest sides facing north and south; and
- solar gain in winter.

Outdoor living spaces should be protected in summer and exposed to the sun in winter. This can be achieved through use of pergolas, with deciduous creepers or vines, canopies or other forms of retractable cover.

Landscaping the urban space

While good urban design can be a canvas for good architecture, good landscaping is an essential element in the refinement of the whole. Over the centuries, approaches to landscaping have evolved, on the one hand, into highly mannered art forms and, on the other, into benign neglect. There are many variations in between. After the austere age of Classicism, there was a move to break away from strictly applied rules. Romanticism preached the freedom of feelings for the subject and became manifest most clearly in the gardens of the time. The era of the symmetrical, neatly trimmed and structural French garden was followed by the blossoming of the English landscape garden. Natural herbage was the maxim. Soon gardens that grew wild were all the rage – or rather they were planted to look as if they were wild.

Contemporary tendencies are towards free-form layouts. All projects have their own characteristics, where the landscaping would either be subservient to the existing natural environment or on an equal footing with it, thereby influencing the character of an urban space. Apart from effecting a balance in approach, landscape architects have to respond to briefs that can range from the individual residential plot to complete urban settings, thereby presenting significantly different levels of scale, style of expression and character.

As highways, parks and beaches become more crowded, beautiful places and quiet retreats where the urban dweller can relax and enjoy nature become more important to community health. Some cultivated landscapes become renowned internationally not only for their beauty but also for their acquired cultural importance. A case in point is Giverny, France, the garden outside the studio of the painter Claude-Oscar Monet. Picture perfect in its own right, the garden has become a mecca for millions of visitors from around the globe. The formal, colourful garden in front of the house and the informal lily pond, filled by diverting water from the River Epte, are 'living paintings' and the inspiration for the artist's own famous canvases.

Such examples of tranquillity and peace become more difficult to realise in a world where natural resources are being strained to the limit through escalating exploitation. In view of continuing resource destruction, environmental responsibility requires serious commitment to the promotion of biodiversity, involving, for example, the use of indigenous, native plant life in landscaping. All regions around the world have species that have adapted successfully to their own specific climates and these should form the basis for landscaping projects, particularly in arid regions.

Streetscaping

While the quality of urban social space depends on architectural and urban design principles, it is by no means complete without amenities such as fountains, sculptures, street furniture, street lamps and planters for embellishment to humanise otherwise bland voids between buildings and streets. A place to assemble, gather or meander is always enhanced by paying attention to the details of streetscaping.

Whyte (1982) observed certain behavioural patterns in small public spaces, supporting the theory that planned outdoor amenities exert a significant influence on social interaction. Children, in particular, have a better sense of place if the urban neighbourhood contains structured play environments that are scaled to their size and humanised by good landscaping, lighting and well-designed equipment. The quality of the urban environment has an impact on children's conduct and their willingness to learn acceptable social behaviour. Children learn through their senses – a child at play is, in fact, learning and he or she can learn from the environment in a positive way. Barren urban spaces are the antithesis of what is necessary for satisfactory social development, whereas good neighbourhood playgrounds can stimulate multisensory play. If well designed, they can provide the environmental conditions for a child's social intercourse and positive experiential appreciation of the urban habitat.

In the wider public context the urban environment requires planned street amenities comprising many familiar forms, usually under the umbrella of landscape architecture, such as well-designed seating, fountains, shelters, steps, kiosks, street trees and tended plant boxes.

Options for recreational space should include a range for both formal (e.g. organised games) and informal (e.g. play spaces, parks) use.

Fractal design in urban space

Nature presents itself as a complex web of relationships between various parts of a unified whole – the iterating and energetic geometry of fractals at different scales, where components must be defined through interrelationships among one another and the dynamics of the whole system. The study of wholeness is akin to the study of chaos as represented by fractals, and it holds exciting possibilities for new organic design forms in both urban design and architecture. The more prosaic level in urban design and typologies that are scaleable or measurable limit the scope of creating urban spaces that are spiritually, physically and mentally satisfying.

Through nature – and a greater understanding of the intrinsic design cues which emerge – urban design could explore new directions of responsiveness and sustainability.

In nature certain phenomena appear chaotic, with no apparent structure or pattern, thereby eluding conventional linear mathematics. But the apparent chaos has now become legible graphically through a clearer understanding of the nature of fractals and with it 'non-linear' geometry. Mandelbrot (1977) was a pioneer in this field in the 1960s and later described his work in *The Fractal Geometry of Nature*.

Applying the principles of the 'order' underlying apparent chaos found in natural forms to design generally is breathtaking in scope, affording new directions into more natural expressions of structured form. This can be expressed in self-similarity between the scale of the parts and the whole – the hallmark of fractal geometry.

Mandelbrot (1977) argued that in order to appreciate how the points, lines, planes and solids of the real world fill space, the Euclidean idea of distance (and measurement) should be abandoned. He first contemplated what are now called 'linear fractals' which indicate that the lines in the figures stay straight as the iterations proceed. He also discovered that by using 'non-linear' equations, the feedback of iteration that produces a fractal can bend straight lines into curves and swirls, and make the self-similarity at different scales deformed and unpredictable. The non-linear version exists in a purely mathematical form. The third type of fractal introduces a random element to the iteration and allows fractal artists to model the natural roughness or irregularity of waves, clouds and mountains. Therefore, the fractal dimension of any complex, apparently chaotic feature – such as the branching patterns of a tree – can now be determined (Briggs, 1992).

Trees can be plotted fractally in two and three dimensions. Wherever self-similarity is generated across scales by the repetition of a simple branching, tree-like structures emerge, with graphic examples being rivers with visible inflow channels or the routing of nerves and blood flow in the human body. On an urban scale, the structure of many ancient cities is generally tree-like, with radial street systems converging on and growing around a historic centre, likened to fractal carpets (van Niekerk, 1999).

Gleick (1998: 117) describes the influence of fractals on perception in terms of design, stating: "Our feeling for beauty is inspired by the harmonious arrangement of order and disorder as it occurs in natural objects – in clouds, trees, mountain ranges, or snow crystals. The shapes of these are dynamical processes jelled into physical forms, and particular combinations of order and disorder are typical of them." Gleick attributes the development of the notion of 'fractals' to Mandelbrot, who created the noun and adjective, and observed: "art that satisfies lacks scale, in the sense that it contains elements of all sizes." Furthermore, as a departure from Euclidean mathematics, "the new mathematics of fractal geometry brought hard science in tune with the peculiarly modern feeling for untamed, uncivilised, undomesticated nature."

In the post-millennium era there is a widespread belief that there is something in the development of life that cannot be explained in physical terms alone. When considering the ambiguity and intractability of the late twentieth-century city, experience suggests that myriad social and physical complexities of urban life are perceived as mainly negative.

The phenomenon of fractals was ignored as a touchstone for the conscious generation of design until very recently, and to a large extent it has remained unexplored as a basis for aesthetic expression. In its short history of limited application, the proponents of this non-linear mathematical basis for design have achieved significant acclaim from users of their architectural creations. Application of fractal design in urban space could bring about a renaissance through its associations with natural principles and association with the habitat for urban living.

It is widely suggested that design practitioners working on the built environment – a field that has major impacts on global resources and systems – should first determine the 'reach of a place' as the context for the work to follow. In simple terms, this task starts by asking the question: how big is here? The answer is not always immediately apparent, for, as Kelly (1955) notes, wherever you live, your tiny spot is deeply intertwined within a larger place, embedded – fractal-like – into a whole system called a watershed, which is itself integrated with other watersheds in a tightly interdependent biome. Ultimately, your home is a cell in an organism called a planet. All these levels interconnect with one another.

(Kelly, 1955)

References

Alexander, C., Davis, H., Martinez, J. and Corner, D. *The Production of Houses* (New York: Oxford University Press, 1985).

Alexander, C., Ishikawa, S. and Silverstein, M. *A Pattern Language* (New York: Oxford University Press, 1977).

Balkin, J.M. *Cultural Software: A Theory of Ideology* (London: Academic, 1994).

Bentley, I., Alcock, A., Murrain, P., McGlynn, S. and Smith, G. *Responsive Environments: A Manual for Designers* (London: Architectural Press, 1985).

Briggs, J. *Fractals: The Patterns of Chaos: Discovering a New Aesthetic of Art, Science and Nature* (London: Thames & Hudson, 1992).

Caminos, H. and Goethert, R. *Urbanization Primer: Project Assessment, Site Analysis, Design Criteria for Site and Services of Similar Dwelling Environments in Developing Areas* (Cambridge, MA: The MIT Press, 1978).

Chernushenko, D. *Greening our Games: Running Sports Events and Localities that Won't Cost the Earth* (Ottawa: Canada Centurion, 1994).

Ching, F.D.K. *Architecture, Form, Space and Order* (New York: Van Nostrand Reinhold Co., 1979).

Davidson, F. and Payne, G.K. *Urban Projects Manual* (Liverpool: Liverpool University Press, 1983).

Dawkins, R. *The Selfish Gene*, 3rd edition (Oxford: Oxford University Press, 2006).

Fuggle, R.F. and Rabie, M.A. *Environmental Concerns in South Africa* (Cape Town: Juta & Company, 1983).

Gans, H.J. *People and Plans: Essays on Urban Problems and Solutions* (New York: Columbia University Press, 1991).

Gleick, J. *Chaos: The Amazing Science of the Unpredictable* (London: Heinemann, 1988).

Karimi, K. "A Configurational Approach to Analytical Urban Design: Space Syntax Methodology." *Urban Design International* 17 (2012): 297–318.

Kelly, G. *The Psychology of Personal Constructs* (New York: Norton, 1955).

Koenigsberger, O., Ingersoll, T.G., Mayhew, A. and Szokolay, S.V. *Manual of Tropical Housing and Building: Climatic Design Part 1* (London: Longman, 1974).

MacKenzie, A. "Placemaking and Place-led Development: A New Paradigm for Cities of the Future" (n.d.). Available at: www.pps.org/reference/placemaking-and-place-led-development-a-new-paradigm-for-cities-of-the-future/, accessed 30 November 2015.

Mandelbrot, B. *The Fractal Geometry of Nature* (San Francisco: W.H. Freeman, 1977).

Morkel, M.P. "Residential Densities – Quo Vadis." *Housing in South Africa* November (1988): 18.

van Niekerk, P. "Fractal Design in Architecture." Unpublished essay (1999).

Rapoport, A. *Human Aspects of Urban Form* (New York: Pergamon Press, 1977).

Sitte, C. *City Planning According to Artistic Principles* (London: Phaidon Press, 1965).

South African Pocket Oxford Dictionary, 7th edition (Cape Town: Oxford University Press, 1987).

Sudjic, D. *The Edifice Complex: How the Rich and Powerful Shape the World* (London: Penguin, 2006).

Talib, K. *Shelter in Saudi Arabia* (New York: Academy Editions/St Martin's Press, 1984).

Thomas, D.C. *Architecture and the Urban Environment: Holistic Design* (Cape Town: Mercutio Books, 2013).

Whyte, W.H. "Small Space is Beautiful: Design as if People Mattered." *Technology Review* 85(5) (1982): 36–40.

Chapter Seven

Linking planning primers with planning actions

These would vary according to the project outcome and the particular urban space component forming the focus of the methodologcal process.

> *The art of urban design fundamentally lies in the maintenance of a productive dialogue achieved through a process of continual revision of visions and projects without sacrificing their essential qualities and characteristics while also strengthening their qualities, coherence and persuasiveness.*
>
> (Loeckx *et al.*, 2004: 194)

1. Spatial continuity

In the attempt to create a public space which enables social encounter, there are two types of relationships to be considered: between inhabitants and strangers, and among the inhabitants themselves.

Social spaces have been the subject of study by some urban researchers, such as Alexander (1977) and Hillier and Hanson (1984), with the latter describing social spaces as either 'convex' or 'concave'. Convex is achieved if a line connecting any two points around the perimeter of an open space does not go outside that perimeter. This concept of convex zones is seen to create a potential 'field' of social encounters which, when linked axially, can expand to a matrix of interconnections. Developed further, Hillier and Hanson (1984: 26–27) observe that:

> a society does more than simply exist in space. It also takes on a definite spatial form and it does so in two senses. First it arranges people in space in that it locates them in relation to each other, with greater or lesser degree of aggegation and separation, engendering patterns of movement and encounter. Second it arranges space itself by means

of buildings, boundaries, paths . . . so that the physical milieu takes on a definite pattern.

This structuring matrix resonates with Mills' research (1998: 37, 38) by showing "which segments of the open space system are more integrating and which are segregating," and, using these data, "new urban designs can be rigorously assessed in terms of the social encounter/movement patterns they will generate."

Since the layout of a neighbourhood virtually controls the formation of play groups, it has a critical effect on the development of the children of that neighbourhood. The typical suburb with the conventional layout of streets represents a potential hazard to the child and therefore is an inhibiting factor in the child's developmental scope. The indispensable need for connected play among children merits due consideration being given to interconnected social spaces in settlements to promote the child's spontaneous bonding with his or her peers in relative safety.

Alexander *et al.* (1977: 345–346) show that optimum 'connected play' can be achieved where "at least 64 households are connected by a swathe of land that does not cross traffic." This can be achieved by connecting several residential clusters.

Related to the findings of another survey, conducted by Whyte (1982), certain invariants in the behavioural pattern of people in small urban spaces were established. These should be regarded as remedial indicators for social spaces, which encourage the chance for social encounter, vital in a community. Apart from a continuous spatial system to promote social interaction, the provision of wide streets and pedestrian squares needs support (Bentley *et al.*, 1985). The addition of seating and other amenities stands for mobile vendors and open-air exhibitions would enhance the experience of an open space.

2. Pedestrian density

According to Alexander *et al.* (1977), an area is considered lively at 15 square metres per person, while a public square can be regarded as dead at 50 square metres per person. They therefore suggest that, for public squares, courts, pedestrian streets, indeed any place where crowds are drawn together, an estimate should be made of the mean number of people in the place at any given moment (P), then the area should be set at between 150P and 300P square feet (approximately 15P and 30P square metres).

It has been mooted that a square of 30 by 30 metres will begin to seem deserted if there are fewer than 30 people in it, and that there are not many places in an urban context where there will *always* be 30 people. On the basis of the thesis that it is possible to recognise a person's face and be heard across a spatial width of 23 metres, Alexander *et al.* (1977) propose that a public square, except where it serves as the centre of a great city, should be no more than 15 to 20 metres across. This applies only to width; no constraint is necessary in terms of length. With the aim of either encouraging or discouraging social encounter, the issue of appropriate pedestrian density levels needs to be addressed in specific situations.

3. Pedestrian streets

Standing and conversing or simple social intercourse are promoted where pedestrian streets can be incorporated into the urban setting. Alexander *et al.* (1977: 490) hold that for pedestrian streets to function properly two special properties are needed. First, vehicular traffic must be excluded; and, second, "the buildings along the pedestrian street must be planned in a way which as nearly as possible eliminates indoor staircases, corridors, and lobbies, and leaves most circulation outdoors." Furthermore, the most comfortable pedestrian streets are those where the "width of the street does not exceed the height of the surrounding buildings."

In locations where public activity is sufficiently intense, watching other people in itself can become a welcome diversion. Bentley *et al.* (1985) maintain that this mostly happens at the edge of the space which offers a sense of refuge as well as a good view of what is happening. They also suggest that the view could be enhanced if the seating were at a slightly higher level than the space itself. The width of the pedestrian movement zone must be appropriate to the level of pedestrian traffic involved. In some public spaces, social encounter might be regarded as highly important, in which case the choice of either pedestrian-only streets or integrated public spaces is indicated.

Between the movement zone and the vehicular space, allow a zone for amenities such as street trees, seating, bus shelters, telephone kiosks and cycle tracks wherever the need is demonstrated. Parked cars are themselves effective barriers between pedestrians and moving vehicles.

4. Places to linger

In a survey of small New York plazas, Whyte (1982) noted that most downtown squares were not used much except for crossing to the other side. This correlates with the conclusions of other urban design commentators who argue that streets are 'centrifugal' not 'centripetal' and tend to drive people out instead of drawing them in (Alexander *et al.*, 1977), unless the amenity value of the place holds some attraction for them. Both Whyte and Alexander *et al.* proceed from the standpoint that social encounter should be a primary goal. The suggestion is then made that this can be accomplished by shaping the pedestrian streets concave on plan, with well-sited seating and shelter around the perimeter. People like well-defined places and tend to gravitate towards the edge of a public square. If the building edge does not provide them with places where they can linger, the place will become more of a thoroughfare than a social space (Alexander *et al.*, 1977).

Another pattern identified by Alexander *et al.* (1977) is the custom that people have of facing the view or towards whatever there is which comes nearest to a view. People feel most comfortable in spaces that have a 'back' and a 'view into a larger space'. This axiom would apply at all scales – from a seat in a garden to a town square with a vista on to a larger space.

Bentley *et al.* (1985) recommend that the following seating principles will assist in colonising the square and encouraging the distributed use of the space:

- Locate seating parallel to pedestrian flows; on wider streets with active use on both sides, arrange seats down the centre of the space.
- In squares establish desire lines for pedestrian flows and then arrange seating to take advantage of the people-watching potential of these positions. Some people like to stand or lean in similar locations.
- Seating can take the form of primary seating, such as chairs and benches, or secondary features, such as steps, walls and planters. As much primary seating as possible is desirable – never less than 10 per cent of the total number of seats, and 30 centimetres of seating for each 3 square metres of open space is recommended.
- Plan seating configurations to encourage planned or spontaneous encounter.
- Avoid locating seats lower than their surroundings as this reduces their potential prospect on to a larger space.

Having discounted shape and scale as the major determinants in what constitute popular social spaces, Whyte's (1982) survey team examined the amount of 'sittable' space. They found that the most popular plazas tend to have more sitting space than the less well-used ones. Factors such as the actual design of the seating were not considerations, as a ledge or a step would serve as a sitting space equally as well as a seat designed for the purpose. Ideally, seats should be comfortable for the user, preferably with back-rests and well contoured. Socially comfortable sitting choices should be built into the design, allowing people to sit facing other people, or to the side, or back-to-back, in the sun, in the shade, in groups, or alone. Whyte's conclusion was that the ratio of seating area to total area of open space should ideally be around one to ten for the circumstances of the case study.

As activities fill the perimeter of a public space it becomes more lively, so opportunity for pockets of activity should be incorporated into the edge of public spaces and contain spontaneous activities and amenities – attributes that encourage people to linger.

5. Sun/wind controls

In determining the influence of the sun on the popularity of public spaces, Whyte (1982) found that the progress of the seasons, and hence the degree

Image 7.1 Places to linger: waterfront and inner city

of penetration of the sun, correlates with the preference to sit or not to sit in the sun. Therefore, social spaces should not be simple sun-traps but must also have some shade. People should be able to choose whether to sit in full sun or shade, according to preference.

Sunlight is important since people tend to follow the sun across a space, seeking or avoiding it according to the climate. The levels of sunlight and shade can be altered by design adjustments at a variety of scales: building mass, open space width, level changes, trees or other features within the space.

Whyte (1982) also found that the absence of wind and draughts was just as critical as the opportunity to enjoy the sun. Air movements around new buildings can radically alter comfort standards by creating gusting and eddying.

Bentley *et al.* (1985) identify microclimate as an important factor, particularly windspeed and sunlight, in the range of possible activities, and therefore in the 'robustness' (the enabling quality) of a public space, such as for social encounter, vending or recreation. Wind speed is important because it affects temperature. For example, a 50 kilometre an hour wind at –1 degree Celsius has six times the cooling effect of still air at –12 degrees Celsius. The implication is that when urban public spaces are being considered, the designs of the buildings on the periphery are contributory in the following ways:

- Adverse ground-level wind conditions are most frequently associated with buildings that are significantly taller than their surroundings.
- The undesirable micro-effects of wind are more reliably tested through wind-tunnel models of surrounding buildings and building texture beforehand. Such tests can point to improvements that ameliorate impacts on the surrounding open spaces. Mitigation of the unwanted effects of winds can be achieved by the provision of recesses and similar design interventions on the vertical planes enclosing the public space.

6. Colour and texture

Colours affect people emotionally. While such sentient reactions are individual and subjective, Reekie (1972: 19) states that there is evidence that, in general, "certain colours are likely to produce certain feelings and this aspect should receive consideration in regard to external design as well as internal design."

The discrete use of colour and its potential enhancement of the aesthetic appeal of an urban space cannot be overrated. On the basis of empirical observation, Reekie (1972) has commented on the human response to certain colours, listing the most common psychological perceptions of individual colours:

- Blue: soothing effect if not too strong.
- Green: similar in effect to blue.
- Yellow: cheering and stimulating.

- Red: exciting.
- Purple: in small areas, rich and comforting; in large areas, disturbing.
- Browns: restful and comforting.
- White: cheering and stimulating.

Schumacher (1981: 10) promotes the axiom that the simpler the form on which a colour is presented, the more effective that colour will appear to be. As a corollary, colour should be employed "wherever the opportunity to create effects by means of formal articulation has been denied." He points out that John Ruskin first advanced the theory that "form and colour were enemies and should therefore be set on essentially different paths." The highest intensity of colour, in his view, "should never coincide with the highest complexity of form." In view of contemporary cultural trends and changing norms of acceptability, these guidelines should be taken as general but not absolute.

In practice, colourist theories, of which there are many, assist the understanding of the colour spectrum and the principles governing successful employment of colour to evoke expected responses in the viewer.

Before venturing into the realm of colour with a view to using it to enhance environmental quality, it is useful to possess a working knowledge of the nature of colour and chromatic terminology:

- Colour quality is the specific character of colour that arises from the attributes of hue (chromatic colours), degree of lightness (or value), purity (or saturation), intensity and emotional effect.
- Hue is that attribute of a colour by which it can be distinguished from another of the same lightness and purity. Often, based on the arrangement of the colours on a wheel analogous to a compass, a colour's hue is termed its 'direction'.
- Lightness refers to the degree of difference of the colour from black – at the darkest end of the spectrum – and white, at the lightest end.
- Colour purity (or saturation) is that attribute that determines the degree of difference between a certain tone and neutral grey.
- Colour intensity is the strength (or 'power') of a colour; the saturated colours of the colour wheel are perceived as the most intense.
- Both intensity and saturation are diminished by the addition to a colour of white, black or grey. This means that each colour reaches its highest point of intensity and saturation at a different degree of lightness: for example, yellow does so at a higher degree of lightness than blue.
- Saturated colours affect the eye with unequal strength; for example, no saturated green can approach the intensity of saturated red.

The emotional value of a colour arises from the psychophysical effect it has on us, which is at least the result of a certain inherent expressiveness unique to each colour (Olbrich, 1987). Further:

- Directional colour contrast: when two colours on opposite sides of the colour wheel (for example, blue and orange) largely determine the overall composition.
- Light–dark contast: if the central contrast in the composition is light–dark, the values of the colours used will come particularly into play and have a great influence on the overall effect. Here the hues play a secondary role, as they are merely accessories to the light–dark contrast.
- Pure and greyed hues contrast: if the composition is carried out largely in one range of value (or lightness), its effects will rest on the contrasts between pure and greyed hues.
- Cold–warm colour contrast: if the colours belong to the accepted cold or warm part of the spectrum, the predominance of one over the other will create the contrast.
- Single hue compositions: variations of a single hue with accents picked out by contrasting degrees of lightness or darkness.

Colour systems are an essential aid to the designer as they represent classifications devised with great care to include as many variations of colour as possible in a sequence: hue, saturation, lightness and interval. Some go further, such as that published by Schuitema (1965), which provides a number of suggested colour combinations to assist the designer. Colour systems are fine aids to composition as they bring order into the confusion of the colour range. Schumacher (1981) lists the following colour systems:

- Newton's Colour Wheel;
- Mayer's Colour Scheme;
- Lambert's Colour Pyramid;
- Runge's Colour Sphere;
- Benson's Colour Cube; and
- Ostwald's Colour Norm Atlas.

Reekie (1972: 23) states:

> Texture modifies colour. If two surfaces are both of the same hue and intensity, but are of different textures, they will not look alike. Texture can be regarded as the visual impression of what can be experienced by touch . . . the same words e.g. rough, smooth, etc. are used to describe texture whether a surface is seen or felt.

The decorative application of colour and texture should be carried out with a definite aim in mind, whether aesthetic or functional. Colours and textures can be used to articulate, distinguish and enliven surfaces and objects, and so help to enhance the urban social space.

In urban design an important contribution of texture other than aesthetic is that, if used selectively, it can reduce reflectivity and therefore lessen unwanted glare on horizontal as well as vertical surfaces.

Image 7.2 Colour and texture: contemporary and traditional

7. Sensory stimuli

Heath (1984: 112), who has researched visual stimuli in the design and planning of urban social spaces, concludes that "some insights have been provided by research on 'arousal'." Behavioural and neurological evidence suggests that the hedonic or rewarding value of a stimulus depends on how 'arousing' or 'de-arousing' it is. Two distinct mechanisms seem to be involved: one produces reward when stimulation decreases after it has risen to the point of being unpleasant or painful, while the other comes into play when arousal increases to a moderate extent.

Rapoport (1977: 229) raises the notion that 'noticeable differences' are critical to design. He provides a list of cues to which people respond subliminally:

- Physical differences: vision: shape, size, height, colour, materials, texture, details.
- Space: size, shape, barriers, links, merging, transitions.
- Light and shade: levels, temporal changes in light.
- Greenery: man-made versus natural, type of planting.
- Conformity versus variety.
- Well maintained versus neglected.
- Scale and urban grain.
- Road pattern.
- Topography.
- Location: prominence, at junctions.
- Kinesthetics: changes of level, curves, speed of movement.
- Sound: noisy versus quiet; man-made versus natural sounds; dead versus reverberant; temporal changes in sound.
- Smells: man-made versus natural.
- Air movement.
- Tactile.
- Social differences.
- Activity: type and intensity; uniform or mixed; cars or pedestrians; movement or quietude.
- Objects: signs, advertisements, fences, decorations.
- Street use or non-use; front–back distinctions; private–public distinctions; introverted versus extroverted.
- Hierarchy or symbolism.
- Temporal differences: long term versus short term.

8. Proportion

Nowhere do mathematics, science and philosophy permeate aesthetics as significantly as in the problem of space. Although what presents itself as harmonious to one person may not necessarily be similarly described by another. The character of a space or building will inevitably be endowed by its own scale, proportion and form as much as by the quality of the architectural elements involved in its definition as a space or enclosure.

Doczi (1985) has demonstrated that proportional harmonies have been fundamental to spatial philosophy in Japan for centuries. For example, in the Zen Monastery Temple Garden near Kyoto, which dates from the beginning of the fifteenth century, five groups of rocks are placed on a rectangular field of coarse, raked, white sand. This outdoor space is designed to be seen from the veranda of the monastery and from paved walkways around it. In Doczi's (1985: 118) words:

> The field of sand has proportions corresponding to two reciprocal golden rectangles . . . multiple constructions of the golden section show how the distances between the rocks within the field share proportional relationships that correspond to the root harmonies of music. Thus the rocks and field become one.

Typically, subjectivity underlies the appreciation of good proportion and a comfortable scale, but it can also be shown that visual harmony of proportion has mathematical roots. These mathematical roots of proportion have been studied scientifically since the time of Vitruvius in the first century AD and up to more modern times with the development of the golden section concept at the end of the nineteenth century. Unity is to be found in the manifold diversities of nature, brought about by the sharing of the same simple harmonious proportional formula. Doczi (1985: 2) describes the formula derived for the celebrated golden section as a "uniquely reciprocal relationship between two unequal parts of a whole, in which the small part stands in the same proportion to the large part as the large part stands to the whole." An approximation of the golden section is a rectangle of 5 × 8 proportions (Doczi, 1985). It can be defined geometrically as a line that is divided in such a way that the lesser portion a is to the greater b as the greater b is to the whole $a + b$. This can be expressed algebraically by the equation of two ratios: $a/b = b/a+b$.

The complete reciprocity of the golden section proportion strikes the viewer as particularly harmonious and pleasing, a fact that has been proven by many scientific experiments. The phenomenon occurs too frequently to be ignored and could be particularly useful as a maxim for visual repose or a sense of tranquillity in the design of urban social space.

When applying proportion principles to space, certain factors need to be taken into account (Bentley *et al.*, 1985):

- The range of distances from which the various parts of the space can be seen.
- The speed of movement at which the space can be seen.
- The relative numbers of people likely to see a space or building from each different viewing position.

Image 7.3 Architecture: the vertical element in tandem

- The length of time during which each view will be experienced.
- The visibility of the elements has to be assured to sustain the visual richness.

9. Human-related scale

"Man is the measure of all things," according to Protagoras, the Greek philosopher of the fifth century BC. Although the art forms of the West and East are vastly different, they possess a common human unity beyond their surface diversity. This can be substantiated by constructions of harmonious relationships in Hellenic sculpture, with Vitruvius, the Roman architect and writer, demonstrating "that the ancient Greeks even laid out their temples according to human proportions" (Doczi, 1985: 106).

In open space, as in architecture, questions of scale centre mainly on two considerations: the size of the space relative to the human body, which includes other human-scaled elements, such as furniture; and the size of the building elements or controlled forms either constituting the enclosure of that space or standing in that space. Generally, people have to rely on the visual rather than the tactile experience of space, and their experiences are largely based on perceptions of scale.

Of an open space's three dimensions, the vertical scale contributes more emphatically to the sense of scale, as the human eye perceives a change in height more readily than a change in plan dimension. However, this ready appreciation of the vertical scale is not without visual reference to the other dimensions. For instance, a change in height is not easily appreciated in a space with a tight, enclosed ground plan, as the visual effect is foreshortened, which affects the ability to perceive any scale.

Both the texture and colour of enclosing surfaces and the effects of foreshortening of perspective and distance complicate the picture, as indeed does cultural preference.

In architecture and urban design, scale is a concept that is used to compare sizes of, for example, mass, area and distance in relation to other normally recognised and accepted sizes. As both disciplines are primarily concerned with the needs and activities of humans, the standards are mostly derived from anthropometrics and ergonomics. "A design or part of a design can be described as 'in scale' if it conforms with human norms, or as 'large in scale' or 'small in scale' according to its departure from these norms" (Reekie, 1972: 23). Reekie concludes that in urban design, questions of scale arise not only with respect to the planning and design of a building, but also with respect to the juxtaposition of buildings and other structures, the scales of which could be so dissimilar as to produce a discordant visual effect. The solution is not necessarily to impose a standard façade, but to require that a satisfactory relationship should exist between them, including a scale compatible to the collective whole.

On the matter of scale, different levels of movement and complexity should be considered. Driving in a vehicle accelerates time and diminishes a person's capacity to absorb detail in the environment. Pedestrians have a better awareness of place than drivers or passengers on public transport. Therefore, in the urban network, where the motor vehicle determines the speed of movement, levels of complexity and scale other than the human scale should be employed. Rapoport (1977) holds that an environment that is comfortably stimulating when seen from a car becomes monotonously boring on foot. As speed increases, concentration increases, and several other things happen too, as Tunnard and Pushkarev (1963) observe:

- The point of concentration (or focus) recedes from 600 feet at 25 miles per hour to 2000 feet at 65 miles per hour. As a result, elements in the environment must become larger to be noticed or appreciated at all.
- While objects perpendicular to the road become prominent those parallel to it lose prominence.
- Peripheral vision diminishes so that while at 25 miles per hour the horizontal angle is 100 degrees, it reduces to less than 40 degrees at 60 miles per hour. One result is 'tunnel vision', which may induce hypnosis or sleep. Side elements need to be quiet and subdued and perceived subconsciously in the blurred field of peripheral vision, with main features on the axis of vision and the point of concentration periodically moved laterally to maintain attention.
- Foreground detail begins to fade, due to the rapid movement of close objects. The earliest point of a clear view recedes from 30 feet at 40 miles per hour to 110 feet at 60 miles per hour. At the same time detail beyond 1400 feet cannot be seen as it is too small, so the range is between 110 and 1400 feet – a distance that is traversed in 15 seconds. Elaborate detail is therefore both useless and undesirable.

It can be concluded that space perception becomes increasingly impaired at accelerated speed so that near objects are seen, get close and disappear over a very short period of time. Thus, objects tend to 'loom', which is potentially disturbing. Objects or installations that are too close to the road edge, or overhead, or on sudden curves should be avoided.

10. Visual order

The elements of scale, proportion, colour and texture play a part not only severally but collectively. At the start of the last century, researchers, including the Gestaltites, set out to identify environmental properties that influence perception. Gestalt theory states that the underlying principles of 'organisation' form part of the perception process. These principles enable discrete stimuli to be perceived holistically as patterns rather than as separate stimuli (Viljoen *et al.*, 1988).

Four principles of organisation are distinguishable in the theory of visual order: proximity, similarity, continuity and closure. Thus, objects in a space form a group when they are close to one another (the principle of proximity) or when they look the same (the principle of similarity). Gibson (1987) argued for a holistic perception of the environment, and that the perceiver receives patterns of stimulation that are intrinsically meaningful. For example, information about spatial depth depends on the gradient of the textured surface, which seems less coarse or rough as it stretches away. In this way, a holistic perception about spatial depth is experienced.

Camillo Sitte (1965), who wrote more than 100 years ago of the meagre and unimaginative character of modern city plans, devised several proposals for creating visual order to attain character in public squares:

- The centre of a public space should be kept free of clutter.
- Public squares should be enclosed.
- The size and shape of public squares are critical.
- Irregularity is acceptable in the configuration of a public square, and does not necessarily negate visual order.
- The ideal street must form a completely enclosed unit visually.

After a lifetime of observing city spatial relationships and the successful embodiment of the aesthetic in physical form, Sitte's conclusions, although arguably not absolute principles, point to some useful, tested conventions to give visual order to urban open space planning.

Sitte studied 255 churches in the city of Rome, and found that only six were free-standing. Thus, he concluded that the centre of a public square should be kept free of buildings. This is of great importance for buildings because they "achieve their full effect only when they can be viewed from an adequate distance on a plaza that is not too large" (Sitte, 1965: 26), and integration with the site is made possible.

Other examples abound of the successful placement of important buildings on a square with one or more sides related to the perimeter. For example, in Italy: Piazza del Duomo, Piacenza and Vicenza; San Cita, Palermo; Piazza del Santo, Padua. In all of these cases successful perspective is achieved without having deeper space, "so that the façade of the building could be viewed as the backdrop to a stage" (Sitte, 1965: 28).

A street intersection in a public square, common in modern town planning, was the exception rather than the rule in medieval towns, since this would prevent any coherence in the social space. The concept of planning the streets to enter the public square from the corners or at varying angles approximates the patterns followed in many medieval towns. Sitte (1965: 34) identifies the cathedral square of Ravenna as the "purest type of this ingenious system."

The size and shape of the public square are critical. "For the purpose of analysing the relationship that exists between the size and shape of plazas and of the major structures on them," Sitte (1965: 39) identifies two types of square: the 'deep type' and the 'wide type'. The position of the observer in relation to a major building and a good proportion between the size of the public square and that of its buildings are determinants in the search for the ideal resolution.

Sitte (1965: 50) states further that "strict symmetry and geometric exactitude" are unnecessary in the "creation of pictorial and architectonic effects," so irregularity in public squares is acceptable. Old public squares were not conceived on the drawing board "but instead developed gradually *in natura*" – that is, the purposeful design of irregular public spaces must be liberated from mechanical conception on the drawing board. To liberate planning from imposed geometry in no way negates the importance of visual order in planning urban settings. The worst effects of imposed geometry, such as triangular public squares or residues of space, which have no functional or aesthetic advantage, should be avoided. Siena, Italy, has numerous examples of public squares that are irregular on plan and create fine settings for the churches. The aim was to "carve out a deep plaza in front of the church façade and to ensure good vantage points for viewing this major structure" (Sitte, 1965: 50).

Not only the public squares of old towns merit study. There is benefit in scrutinising the disposition of their streets for the spatial order they present. Sitte (1965) states that the ideal street must form a completely enclosed unit – the more one's impressions are confined within it, the more perfect its tableau will be. One feels at ease in a space where one's gaze cannot be lost in infinity.

11. Structured urban space

Before the rapid urbanisation of the late twentieth century, places that looked important *were* important, and places of public relevance could easily be identified. Some urban designers link the notion of familiarity with legibility, which is the quality that makes a place graspable. Furthermore, legibility is likely to be important at two levels: in terms of physical form and activity patterns. Generally:

- The biggest open spaces should be related to the most important public facilities.
- The point of a legible layout is that people are able to form clear, accurate images of it. Note that it is the user, not the designer, who forms the image.

Lynch (1981), who pioneered the use of image maps in the 1960s, suggested that there are overlapping features among people's images of places: namely, nodes, edges, paths, districts and landmarks. It would be wrong to assume that every area contains all of these features.

Planners sometimes refer to 'hard' and 'soft' spaces (Trancik, 1986). Both terms have useful functions and contribute to the identity of place in the urban situation:

- Hard spaces are principally bounded by architectural walls. Often they are intended to function as major gathering places for social activity.
- Soft spaces are dominated by the natural environment, whether inside or outside the city.
- Architecture and landscape architecture must respond to and, if possible, enhance environmental identity and sense of place.

Researchers of the city social space environment comment on the notion of 'place' and the associations with the continuity of time that people have with places:

- Part of the presence of any good place lies in the perceived connections: roads with buildings, buildings with buildings, and with trees, the seasons, decorations, events, and other people in other times (Smithson, 1967).
- Just as each locality should seem continuous with the recent past, so it should seem continuous with the near future (Lynch, 1981).
- A place is a space that has a distinct character. Since ancient times the *genius loci*, or spirit of place, has been recognised as the concrete reality man has to face and come to terms with in his daily life (Norberg-Shulz, 1971).
- The character of a place consists of both the concrete substance having shape, texture and colour and the more intangible cultural associations – a certain patina given by human use over time (Trancik, 1986).

These associations of people make demands of timelessness on the urban spaces of their experience, which place a particular onus on the urban planner and designer to enable the bonding of the urban dweller with the urban environment.

The need to have a stable system of places in which urban dwellers may live their social lives and experience their culture gives space an emotional content. Trancik (1986: 112) urges the urban designer "to create truly unique contextual places" and to "explore the local history, the feelings and the needs of the populace, the traditions of craftsmanship and indigenous materials, and the political and economic realities of the community."

Trancik (1986) provides three theories of urban spatial design on the basis of his research into the evolution of modern space and his analysis of historic precedents:

- The Figure–Ground Theory: founded on the relative land coverage of buildings as solid mass (figure) to open voids (ground). The objective is

Image 7.4 Structured space with territorial markers and formal gardens

to manipulate the relationships by adding to or subtracting from, or changing the physical geometry of, the pattern. The Figure–Ground Theory is a graphic tool for illustrating mass–void relationships and a two-dimensional abstraction in plan view that clarifies the structure and order of urban spaces.

- The Linkage Theory: derived from lines formed by streets, pedestrian-ways, linear open spaces connecting one element to another. Movement systems and efficiency of the infrastructure take precedence over patterns of defined outdoor space.
- The Place Theory: goes beyond the other two theories in that it adds the components of human need within cultural, historical and natural contexts. The unique forms and details of a place's indigenous setting add richness.

Trancik states that each of these approaches has merit, but ideally one should draw on all three: give structure to solids and voids, organise links between parts, and respond to human need through indigenous cultural associations with a place.

12. Sense of place

The well-established Western city form – characterised by urban sprawl, in which residential, commercial, recreational and shopping functions are zoned in separate areas – positively disperses feelings of territorial attachment and does not allow a sense of place to develop easily. The manifestation of suburbia maximises privacy to the detriment of other perceived spatial quality attributes. A tighter urban fabric, as suggested by some of the traditional settlement forms, offers social opportunity through the integration of activities, thereby generating vitality and character. It is therefore necessary to look at the validity and potency of high-density urban environments where intrinsically the sense of belonging and the sense of place are more achievable, without sacrificing the experiential appreciation of urban living.

The Western experience is that a human group of more than 1500 people cannot readily coordinate itself to reach decisions about which factors affect their interests. Some set the figure as low as 500. Population thresholds are important in effective social bonding. Evidence suggests that:

- People identify with neighbourhoods that have very small populations.
- Such neighbourhoods are small in area.
- A major road through a neighbourhood destroys it.

In the United States research shows the optimum physical area of a neighbourhood is thought to be between one and three blocks around one's own house. A more significant factor, however, is that a "neighbourhood can only have a strong identity if it is protected from heavy traffic . . . People will not feel comfortable in their houses unless a group of houses forms a cluster, with the public land between them jointly owned by all the householders" (Alexander *et al.*, 1977: 82, 198).

In another survey of 149 people in Levittown, New York, Gans (1991) found that all of them were engaged in some pattern of regular visiting with their neighbours. This is interesting in that it underscores the fact that people want be part of a neighbourhood cluster. The extent to which the opportunity to visit would be utilised in the neighbourhood would depend on cultural and socio-economic factors. On a typical block each home is at the centre of its own cluster, demonstrating that the social patterning continues even when the block layout and neighbourhood plan do not encourage social cluster units and promote anonymity.

To replace a gridlike array of houses on a street, Alexander *et al.* (1977) propose a new type of layout, more personal in nature, which would give people immediate and effective control over their common land. Such a layout responds to the spontaneous preference of people to form a cluster. This is borne out even in the conventional houses-on-street situation, where it has been shown that the "homes immediately around one's own home are the most important" and form an "obvious and tribal-like cluster" (Alexander *et al.*, 1977: 198). Alexander *et al.* (1977: 198) continue: "A cluster is a dynamic social structure, which takes physical shape, and is governed, above all, by the common land at its heart, and by the fluidity of the relations between the individual families and this common land." Therefore, control over the common land reinforces the community and is a worthwhile objective for residential settings.

Even on the conventional street pattern, the concept of clustering emerges as desirable. Alexander *et al.* (1977) identified the following criteria on the basis of keeping in touch, and meeting for decision-making:

- the clusters seem to work best if each has between eight and twelve houses;
- more than twelve houses and the balance is strained;
- in all cases common land which is shared by the cluster is an essential ingredient; and
- ownership is essential for the clustering pattern to take hold, and shared ownership of the social space reinforces the common interest.

Alexander *et al.* recommend that houses should be arranged in very rough but identifiable clusters of eight to twelve households around some common land and paths. The clusters should also be arranged so that anyone can walk through them without feeling like a trespasser.

Clustering in a residential sense is a spatial patterning phenomenon observed throughout history where there is no interference. Rapoport (1977: 254) observes that it is a process which "tends to occur in cities based on perceived homogeneity, differing interpretations of environmental quality, lifestyles, symbol systems, and defences against overload and stress." In Africa, in rapidly urbanising populations, there is a tradition of demarcating territory in the form of clusters on the bases of place, age, occupation, home-ownership, recency of arrival and tribal origin.

The reason for clustering, according to Rapoport (1977) and others, is that with greater facility it enables mutual help, assimilation and urbanisation and the preservation of certain institutions. Clustering tends to maintain and recreate networks, and to strengthen cultural patterns. These common denominators emerge from the research. Clustering as a planning principle could add signficantly to a 'sense of place' on a larger scale.

A rare feature in modern town planning practice is the introduction of a main gate to a housing precinct for the prime purpose of heightening the distinctiveness of the area or its place identity. Alexander *et al.* (1977: 278) propose that "every boundary in the city which has important human meaning – the boundary of a building cluster, a neighbourhood, a precinct –" should be marked by "great gateways where the major entering paths cross the boundary."

13. Cultural identity

Goffman, in *The Presentation of Self in Everyday Life* (1959) and in his subsequent development of this theme, discusses the use of environments as stage sets and props to assist people in enacting their social roles and in escaping from them.

African colonial cities show varied cultural landscapes. Rapoport (1977: 353) describes such cultural landscapes as:

> European suburbs and central areas, workers' camps, Indian and Arab areas, African elements of great variety, depending on origin and culture and using different materials, but all somewhat village-like, dispersed, animated, noisy, colourful with commerce everywhere: a profusion of shops, markets, stalls, stands and workshops, so that no lane or street was without them. At the same time activity shifts among areas – at dawn it is the central market, in the afternoon the small local outdoor markets in each quarter, then shifting markets as itinerant merchants stop on any piece of open land.

It follows that if urban form is an expression of culture, then, as Rapoport (1977: 354) states, "the city is ideally a series of areas of varied culture and subculture character," and a number of design consequences follow:

- It is necessary to understand the cultures of the various groups involved and the influences on form of their values, lifestyles and activity systems.
- The goal is conflict resolution on an urban scale.

Image 7.5 Sense of place with experiential choice

- Use open-ended design with some frameworks that link and relate them. Open-ended design ideally creates environments that allow more degrees of cultural expression.
- Forcing people to modify and evolve is as bad as having no ability to do so.
- Urban social spaces should permit freedom of action, involvement, active–creative adoption and modification.

In older cities of the Western world, squares are far more than square metres of open space. In Italy, Sitte (1965) observed, they are truly social spaces and represent a way of life, a concept of living, and cultural symbolism. The Italian piazza is not only an extension of the citizens' living space; it also expresses "the mediaeval concept of highly enclosed space of picturesque rather than emotional charm" or "the sophisticated and mathematical centralism of the static Renaissance" or "the dynamic feeling of mass movement in space of the Baroque" (Kidder-Smith, 1954: 44–46). In most instances, the spatial forms express the dignity of man with strong cultural symbolism. There is thus also a timelessness and therefore a secure feeling of continuity in the social space settings.

The Greek view of man's relationship to the world is most readily seen in concrete form, especially in Hellenic architectural structures. When describing the Parthenon in its setting on the Acropolis, Wheeler (1964: 12) noted: "Neither the building nor its decoration had any inner life; it was a perfect exterior, a perfect piece of man-made geology." Just as the sacred ceremonies occurred outside the buildings, so the structures themselves turn outwards with their pedimental sculpture. In this way the Greek culture was expressed in social spaces that offered opportunity in a responsive way.

Rapoport (1977: 356) refers to open-ended design as "a form of design which determines certain parts of the system, allowing other parts, including unforeseen ones, to happen spontaneously." Enabling environments thus allow a level of meaning to be given through personalisation and through the opportunity for expressing different values, needs and lifestyles. This approach overcomes the problem of a 'tight fit'. Open-endedness and cultural landscapes imply an active role of people in the urban environment. Rapoport (1977: 368) argues that, given an opportunity, people will choose an appropriate environment for themselves and that "this is the most important way in which people assert a sense of mastery and control over their environment and that is an important factor in their well-being."

14. Efficient mobility

Movement patterns or perceptible desire lines forming the traffic arteries of a village, town or city present opportunities that can be exploited. Whether configurations are linear, a grid or random system connecting nodal points, a radial system or spiral, the resultant richness of spatial diversity at the intersections can be well exploited to promote social interaction and economic activity.

Depending on the type of mobility, such as motor vehicle, bicycles or pedestrians, it is important that the traffic movement is not inhibited, but also that it should not destroy the integrity of a public space with which it links and through which it passes. Planning can employ devices such as a mediating space to avoid the complete bisection of a space by a movement system. Alternatively, a movement system could pass through axially, obliquely or along the edge of a space. A movement system can also be planned to terminate in a space.

Essentially, the three-dimensional form of a movement system comprises attributes that relate to:

- The expected performance of the path of movement as part of a system of circulation. The width and height of a circulation space are functions of the type and amount of traffic it must handle.
- The form of the spaces through which it passes.
- The entrances which open on to a space.
- Considerations of scale, proportion, light and vistas.
- The degree of enclosure – complete, open on one side or open on both sides.
- The manner in which changes in level are handled.

The Brazilian city of Curitiba – comprising about 1.6 million people – has taken the lead in organising a particularly rational public transport system. Its unique 'surface metro' is a highly efficient network of fast-running buses, obviating the need for an underground system. The city has built high-speed bus lanes that mean the buses are not held up by car traffic. With a bus stop every 400 metres, citizens have convenient access to buses, and cylindrical loading tubes that allow passengers to pay their fares in advance speed up the boarding process. Curitiba's public transport system is used daily by 1.3 million passengers, and it is faster and often cheaper than those of other Brazilian cities. The city also has an extensive system of cycle lanes, as well as traffic-calming measures in selected streets. Despite high car ownership (one car for every five people), car use is lower in Curitiba than in most other Brazilian cities.

> *New York has taken a close look at Curitiba's surface metro system and hopes to make its own bus routes more efficient. A high-speed bus network could serve to improve linkages between the various transportation systems currently in use in the New York metropolitan region.*
>
> (Girardet, 1992: 150)

15. Functionality

To achieve safe, convenient and rewarding social spaces that function independently, collectively, formally or informally, post-Radburn developments have led to attempts to provide street users, particularly children, with a more informal, human-scale environment. Baker *et al.* (1985: 248) observe that in recent developments there has been a conscious drive to create in vehicle drivers "the feeling of an intruder in a pedestrian domain. In order to accomplish this, careful attention has to be given to the road layout of an estate." The following counter-measures are features that have been identified as central to the success of the post-Radburn concept and the safety of the pedestrian:

- A road hierarchy in the neighbourhood eliminating through traffic.
- Narrow, even circuitous, carriageways.
- Materials and textures more associated with pedestrian areas – cobbles, brick paving and less conventional road surfaces.
- Shared pedestrian/vehicle access ways or 'shared spaces' and an absence of pavements. As a form of zoning, this might suggest separate provision for pedestrians and vehicles and signal vehicle priority to a driver.
- Reduced visibility.
- Short vistas.
- Rumble strips.

The post-Radburn layouts offer more safety and flexibility of trafficways to all users, particularly children. Moreover, as part of the social space system, they enable designers to create higher-quality residential environments by eliminating a disproportionate amount of hard surfaces.

Another development towards the successful integration of functions in a street is the application of the *woonerf* concept to existing streets, typical in parts of Holland and Germany. This concept combines traffic management through physical constraints in the residential street with increased space for play, socialising and leisure. The livability of existing neighbourhoods is thereby enhanced. Studies of the impact of *woonerven* on leisure activities have shown that the chief benefit has been an increase in children's play. "Although verbal communication among grown-ups did not increase with the redesign of the streets, the latter did have an effect on areas where communication took place." On the other hand, because of increases in the length of time spent on the streets, Eubank-Ahrens noted a corresponding increase in the amount of interaction: "children (and, indirectly, their parents) seemed to feel more secure, allowing for a proliferation of types of play" and "children gained more contact with adults, which would not have been possible in playgrounds or other isolated play facilities" (Eubank-Ahrens, 1987: 63).

Woonerven clearly provide more behaviourial options for children at their home base, and thus contribute to social space quality. The integration of functions in a form similar to *woonerven* can potentially improve the functionality of the urban spatial system by enhancing its efficiency as a movement corridor and a social space simultaneously. However, some negative contacts also occurred: "In changing neighbourhoods, conflicts invariably arise between the established older order and newly arrived residents," while "the different behaviour of various age groups . . . [has] an impact on the usability of public open space" (Eubank-Ahrens, 1987: 76).

Shared spaces are only possible where traffic flows are below 250 vehicles per hour, and when the majority of vehicles' final destinations are in the area itself. No area of streets designed on the 'shared space' principle should be more than 500 metres from a 'normal' vehicular street. Also:

- Each street in the area should have directional changes every 50–60 metres, but additional changes might be necessary.
- Two-way traffic should be encouraged throughout the area, to reduce vehicle speed.
- The section should be kept narrow, with occasional widening.
- Raised objects should be lower than 750 millimetres, to allow good visibility for motorists in case of play activity on the street.
- Adequate on-street parking for residents and visitors must be provided. This demands greater attention from drivers, and provides better play spaces in the absence of parked cars.

In a busy vehicular street, the pedestrian movement zone should be given special consideration appropriate to the level of pedestrian traffic involved. A zone for amenities can be created in subtle ways, such as street trees, seating, bus shelters, telephone kiosks and cycle racks. Not all of these can be justified in all situations, but space should be left for others to be added later.

In Woodstock, Cape Town, Dewar and Uytenbogaardt (1977) found that private outside spaces in general were extremely limited. Because backyard spaces were small and usually functioned as surplus storage areas, family activities often spilled into the public space and thus into the community life of the area.

On noisy, heavily trafficked streets, seclusion and quiet can be improved by setting buildings back from the street boundary. To maintain a good relationship with the street, these setback spaces fronting on dwellings should be raised above street level.

Sharing facilities, such as the multifunctional utilisation of school sports grounds, warrants consideration. Morkel (1988) suggests that significant enhancement of opportunity in the residential environment can be achieved by:

- The integrated design of residential environments for the more productive use of space. Through careful design, greater proportions of streets can, for example, be integrated into the housing environment as community social space.

- Through more open-ended zoning practices, local shopping and commercial facilities could be integrated into the residential environment in order to obviate the need for setting aside specific sites for these facilities. The practice of including shopping at ground level with residential accommodation above could be encouraged as a further option.
- Alternative housing options should be explored. Research conducted into residential densities in cities across the world indicate that socially efficient patterns emerge regarding the relationship of high-density residential environments and the use of the courtyard house form. More recently this house form has received increasing attention in contemporary contexts, such as Alexander's proposed housing in Lima, Peru; research at Cambridge led by Martin and March (1972); recent housing projects in parts of Manhattan and Los Angeles; and many housing estates in Britain, the Netherlands and Sweden.

The courtyard house, an alternative form of housing, demonstrates the merits of perimeter development of a site. Morkel (1988: 21) refers to the configuration as "a particularly efficient housing option" generally relating to large-scale housing complexes. In outline, the merits of the courtyard house and perimeter development are:

- High densities can be achieved while still affording ready access to outdoor space.
- The spaces encapsulated within the built form lend themselves to easy integration into the community, thus promoting community interaction, privacy, defensibility and surveillance by residents.

As an alternative, layouts comprising very small plots should show consideration for the long term, where the extension of individual house units could raise issues among neighbhours.

16. *Optimum density*

Practical experience indicates that at the early stages of a design, three simple tests should be applied critically to avoid the wasteful use of scarce land resources that would result in unnecessary expense and increased burdens on the user and public service agencies.

The test criteria are Land Utilisation Index (LUI), Network Length/Area Index and Density, which provide a framework for evaluating early design densities and layout proposals.

The LUI, proposed by Caminos and Goethert (1978: 279), defines the "qualification of the land around a dwelling in relation to user, physical controls and responsibility." In this context, four types of land are identified: public, semi-public, private and semi-private. The LUI is derived from three separate scenarios:

- The actual user, from the individual in a private lot to undefined groups in public streets.
- The responsible agent, such as the public sector in streets and the individual user in a lot.
- The type and means of control, ranging from legal and social controls to physical barriers, such as fences.

To illustrate the application of the third parameter, for example, the addition of a fence or buffer zone increases control and may change the actual use of a piece of land to semi-public status from purely public.

The Network Length/Area Index is the ratio of the length of the network to the area(s) contained within or tangentially to it. It is determined by measuring the total area served by a network, and the length of the network itself. Units are expressed in length per unit area, such as metres per hectare.

Density is generally defined as the ratio between the population of a given area and the area itself. It can be in terms of either: gross density, which encompasses all land use components; or net density, which refers to the population ratio using only the residential land component and does not include land set aside for other purposes.

A graphic representation of these indices for the various scenarios would be useful for evaluation and comparison, and for estimating the costs of utilities – street paving, water distribution networks, sewage disposal networks and electrical lines – and non-physical services, such as refuse collection. In general terms, the lower the ratio, the more cost effective the network, assuming that its basic service functions are maintained.

17. Building interfaces

Buildings that do not create the possibility of a connection with the world outside do not invite the public near and present an image of being aloof and essentially private territory exclusively for the people who are inside (Alexander *et al.*, 1977). Such buildings add nothing to the urban dweller's quality of life. Through negotiation, an attempt should be made to enhance the social amenity value of the periphery of an urban space by paying attention to existing and new building frontages and the extent to which they can enhance the inviting and enabling qualities.

With building frontages on to public spaces it is advantageous if "the public edge of the building should house activities which benefit from interaction with the public realm, and can contribute to the life of the public space itself" (Bentley *et al.*, 1985: 63). There are principles for optimising this relationship:

- Locate as many entrances as possible in such positions that comings and goings are directly visible from the public space.
- Encourage any compatible uses within the buildings to spill out into the public area. This principle applies to uses mainly on the ground and first floors.
- Even if there are no specific uses, most buildings contain activities that can contribute to the animation of the public space itself.
- It is still necessary to preserve the privacy of the indoor activity so that the users will not feel the need to screen themselves totally from the public space. Privacy can be achieved by horizontal distance, a change in level and/or a combination of the two.
- The usefulness of the edge is important for people-watching and is greatly increased by providing places to sit.

As there is often no strong connection between the internal functions of a building and the public setting outside, this could cause a dysfunction. The classic solution is the arcade, according to Alexander *et al.* (1977), provided that:

- The public path to the building itself becomes a place that echoes the character of the inside.
- It is covered and becomes an extension to the building by at least two metres.
- The edges of the ceiling are not too high.
- In some situations where it can be achieved, an arcade could pass right through a building.
- Arcades fronting on to spaces where spontaneous and informal trading can take place should be considered to utilise this opportunity to fullest advantage.

In their comparative analysis of urbanism in Cape Town, Dewar and Uytenbogaardt (1977) explore the concept of interface and its application in a representative area. Among others, they identify one factor of critical importance for the quality of the area as a whole – the relationship between public and private space. As a consequence, "The interface between these spaces contributes substantially to the positive nature of this interdependence and plays a number of roles . . . [by having] a fundamental effect on the quality and manner of usage of the other" (Dewar and Uytenbogaardt, 1977: 11).

In the public setting and residential domain, a variety of building types is possible, which generates a variety of public and private interface relationships. Dewar and Uytenbogaardt (1977: 11) observe that what takes place in this public and semi-private space affects the performance of any living area, and "consequently the entire space should be viewed in terms of its social function – it should be regarded as social space."

18. Accessibility

After examining the agoric planning of the ancient Greek civilisation, Peck (1982: 333) observed that few observers seem to recognise that the "glory that was Greece" was made possible by a special form of town planning – that is, the provision of an agora located at the centre of each Greek city. The agora was the place where the inhabitants gathered for political, commercial and social business, so it became the city's living heart.

In the planning of the city's outdoor spaces, the potential social amenity of spaces external to buildings can be greatly enhanced through what could be termed 'agoric planning' and the application of the following principles:

- Comprehensiveness: the agora should contain all of the common amenities for active recreation, within reason, for both sexes, all age groups and all interest and activity groups.
- There should be a centralisation of amenities.
- Attractor planning principles could be followed, such as that based on 'cumulative attraction'.
- Planning using biopoint, biopattern and biodistance principles that record a community's biopoints on a map, joins them up, and shows a collective biopattern. Biodistance that the community has to travel to visit all biopoints will determine the viability of an urban space project.

Peck (1982) maintains that agoric planning is essential to the wellbeing of modern man because it enriches the individual by enriching his or her environment through responsive planning.

19. Personal space

All animals, including man, exhibit behaviour that is commonly known as territoriality. In so doing, the senses are used to distinguish between one space or distance and another. The specific distance chosen depends on a transaction – the relationship between interacting individuals, how they feel, and what they are doing (Hall, 1966). This hypothesis lies behind the four-part proxemic classification system based on the observations of both animals and men. The simplest form of the 'situational personality' is that associated with responses to intimate, personal, social and public transactions. Some people never develop the public aspects of their personalities, while others have trouble with the intimate and personal zones that require

Image 7.6 Flexible use of urban space

toleration of closeness with others. Proxemic classification has been explored as follows:

- Intimate distance: at this distance, the presence of another person is unmistakable and may at times be overwhelming because of heightened sensory inputs. Researchers divide intimate distance into two phases: close and far (15 and 45 centimetres).
- Personal distance: this distance can be represented as a protective sphere that an organism maintains between itself and others. In the close phase (45 to 75 centimetres), physical contact is possible if so desired, but separation is equally viable. Keeping someone at 'arm's length' is one way of expressing the far phase (75 to 125 centimetres) of personal distance.
- Social distance: the boundary line between the far phase of personal distance and the close phase of social distance serves as the 'limit of domination'. Impersonal business occurs in the close phase (125 to 215 centimetres). In the far phase (215 to 365 centimetres) business is conducted in a more formal manner.
- Public distance: in the close phase of public distance (365 to 800 centimetres) an alert subject can take evasive or defensive action. In the far phase (800 centimetres or more), much of the non-verbal part of communication comprises gestures and body stance. The whole man can be seen as quite small, and he is perceived in a setting.

Proxemic behaviour is culturally conditioned and entirely arbitrary. However, it is an important phenomenon of personal space, the need for privacy and an escape from stress to contribute to the planner's understanding of human reaction to personal distance zones.

20. Neighbourhood scale

Communities exist in the minds of city dwellers, and there is often agreement about their boundaries and their stereotyped characteristics. Communities are also important to strengthen a sense of belonging.

Elements of settlement design can reinforce an agreed image of community by means of separation, the placement of local centres, the diversion of main trafficways, the exploitation of irregularities of terrain and other differentiations of physical character.

The creation of common land for the neighbourhood is in keeping with the concept of clustering, and assists the gradations of publicness to which the urban setting is exposed. Alexander *et al.* (1977) promote the idea that a clear distinction should be made between three kinds of home: those in quiet backwaters, where there are twisting paths; those on busy streets; and those in between. Each neighbourhood should have an equal number of each type. Since "the basic issue is one of control," Lynch (1981: 248) questions whether neighbourhoods should be strengthened and reinforced by spatial form, which would allow the urban dweller's options to range from escape from stress to social interaction.

Another device to create a psychological shield against overexposure of a neighbourhood to public activity is the main gateway into a cluster. The gateway should be solid and visible from every line of approach, and could even comprise a hole through a building.

Alexander *et al.* (1977) raise the image of the neighbourhood square as a public outdoor room – a partly enclosed place, possibly with a structure without walls – that is useful for and maintained by the community.

21. Territorial needs

The territorial needs of the individual or the group as expressed in the earlier thematic analysis is instrumental in the development of group and place identity, such as in the ethnic enclaves that are frequently found in larger cities. Population size will effectively threaten the territorial boundaries of the individual, especially in high-density settings, and is associated with the potential carrying capacity of an urban setting without overcrowding.

There is an obverse side to the question of providing for territorial needs. Corporate business's territorial needs differ from those of individuals in that the former aims to project an image of prosperity and is not primarily restricted by barriers of ownership. "The very idea of fitting modestly into the collective city is antithetical to corporate aspirations and the chest-beating individualism of the American way" (Trancik, 1986: 17). As a result, the public space, which is a public good, is inclined to be turned over to private enterprise for development, usually with conditional usufruct attached. Trancik (1986) argues that this process transforms the city of collective spaces into a city of private icons.

Rapoport (1977: 259) observes that open-endedness is also intimately linked with territoriality since it allows personalisation, which is an important way of defining individual and group domains. By allowing group signs to develop this also helps to define rules of occupance, which are then not only noticed and understood, but willingly obeyed. Since these rules are subtle and frequently understated, and also change subtly, the urban designer is not able to provide for them – they are best allowed to develop within an open framework and they can then also respond to change in the population of the various areas. It is a principal way of giving to the environment.

22. Pollution-free social space

Transportation-related air pollutants and their spatial and temporal distribution differ greatly from place to place within the city. Air pollution is a function of commuting patterns, traffic volumes and speed, topography of urban form, built materials and meteorological conditions. A multi-disciplinary understanding of these functions is advisable among practitioners who shape the urban space.

Spirn (1987: 310–319) identifies causes which, once understood, could lead to effective initiatives, including control over building form to open space relationships:

- In flat, open terrain under calm conditions, air pollution levels are highest adjacent to the road and decrease with distance from it.
- Street canyons lined with buildings of similar height and oriented perpendicular to the wind direction tend to have poorer circulation than street canyons that are lined with buildings of different heights and interspersed with open areas. To promote air circulation in street canyons, buildings should be stepped back from the street, openings increased and building heights varied.
- Wind shadows on the lee of buildings reduce air circulation, allowing pollutants to accumulate. To reduce wind shadow at the base of a building, a pyramidical shape or openings that permit air flow should be considered.
- The more enclosed the space, the more likely the accumulation of pollutants. High canopies promote air circulation in streetside arcades.

Highway embankments and woodland growth help filter pollutants from the air during photosynthesis and therefore reduce the effects of pollution. Pollution-sensitive uses should be located away from highway emission zones.

The relation of smog to urban sprawl is well known. "The more sprawl, the greater the energy expended in getting people and materials back and forth between them, and so the greater the air pollution" (Dantzig and Saarty, 1973: 7). As green spaces reduce dust and other pollutants, they contribute to healthier urban settings and consequently to the wellbeing of urban dwellers. The aim should be to achieve a 'safe' urban environment so that people breathe pure air and feel free to utilise the outdoors without concern for their health.

Other forms of pollution – such as noise pollution – have the potential to detract from spatial quality and should be addressed scientifically, particularly when integrated functions are contemplated.

23. Monitoring measures

Community life in the suburbs has too often been found wanting. Street life, even with its hustle and bustle and unstructured supervision, has some attributes that help in the successful raising of chidren, according to Jane Jacobs (1961). The practices of fencing in homes and gardens (for privacy and protection) and of using motor cars for every errand effectively isolate the family from personal encounters with others who live in the neighbourhood. Such environments do not provide guarantees against crime.

In high-density settings, it is possible to provide a spatial system which ensures that the potential presence of others either living in the street or in transit through it help to maintain a sense of security. The governing principle is that important foci – such as the point of entry into a neighbourhood or meeting points along axes within the complex – should be visible for surveillance by the residents themselves. Such a system allows strangers access, but also serves as an effective mechanism for policing the communal space. Hillier and Hanson (1984) maintain that this is a more subtle form of security than a simple grouping of dwellings, and is usually expected to produce a self-policing environment.

24. Street vending space

Opportunity should be created within the system of social spaces to promote economic activity. Social spaces have the potential to play an important role in informal and occasional activities that are important to urban life, such as public meetings, spontaneous theatre, periodic markets, fairs and circuses and so on.

According to Rapoport (1977: 357),

> Most planners conceive of the street as a transitional space and do not allow for it to act as an open space, activity space, or social space, yet it can play an immensely important role in the design and planning of many cities, as we have seen in Mexico, Africa and elsewhere.

Some commentators conclude that the social and commercial roles of the traditional street have been undermined by such design features as enclosed malls, which "have siphoned shopping and entertainment off the street, which no longer functions as a gathering place" (Trancik, 1986: 10). Often these upmarket emporia are situated on the fringes of urban areas and cannot be reached on foot. In this way, they complicate access to the market and tend to exclude the less affluent.

Trafficways and nodal intersections can provide important venues for small trading enterprises, not requiring large capital sums for infrastructure or accommodation, as long as they are designed to enable such activities to take place there. By enabling trading activity, such venues can add colour to the street culture and increase income options, not only for the more needy.

The most humane cities are always full of street cafés. Alexander *et al.* (1977) consider streets, parks, squares, promenades and avenues as essential spatial components so that people can mix in public. The street café is special to cities where, even on busy streets, the front of the café spills on to the pavement with sets of tables and chairs. Mobile food vendors should be accommodated so that public seating can be utilised to enjoy a snack while seated. Alexander *et al.* (1977) propose some rules for food stands, including:

- They should be concentrated at road crossings where they can easily be seen.
- They should be free to take on the character of the area around them.
- They can be portable stands, built into the fronts of buildings or mobile carts.

Alexander *et al.* (1977) also observe that "as the decentralisation of work becomes more and more effective, the workshop in the home grows and grows in importance." The relationship between a workshop and a public street is special, and a potential means to enlarge the connection between the worker and the community. Every member of the community will benefit from this, provided that the workshop can be seen from the street and that the owner can 'hang out a shingle'.

25. Nodes of activity

The economic or physical means to close the distance and ease access to facilities is usually the privilege of the affluent in the modern city, which, by nature of its sprawl, necessitates rapid modes of transport. Dewar (1984: 27–28) considers the "basic unit of performance measurement" and concludes that the primary unit is the "range of opportunities, experiences and activities to which inhabitants of a settlement have easy access." Also, the unit of measurement must be defined in terms of the mobility of the poor of the community – access by people on foot. "If essential city facilities and opportunities are so located and dispersed through space that they are easily available to the poor as well as the wealthy, the entire system is richer."

People want to be close to shops and services, for excitement and convenience; but they also want to be away from services for quiet relaxation (Alexander *et al.*, 1977). To achieve a balance, a gradient of density is proposed. It is held that community facilities scattered individually through a city do nothing for the life of that city. For that reason, nodes of activity should be provided. A small public square should be created at the centre of each node, surrounded by a combination of community facilities and shops that are mutually supportive. The objective is to increase the vitality of the urban setting.

A feature of older cities is the promenade. The relationship between the catch basin of the promenade and the paved area of the promenade itself is critical. Alexander *et al.* (1977: 737) developed a formula for determining

Image 7.7 Street vending: typical across continents

requisite catch basin size with the qualification that "a promenade will not work unless the pedestrian density is high enough."

The average urban dweller demands centres of night life. A cluster of night spots will create life in the street. Other public places surrounded by night-life amenities should be well lit, safe and lively. The clustering of amenities will increase the intensity of pedestrian activity at night by drawing many people to the same few spots in the town. Transport terminals are places for people waiting to embark on public transport, or to be met by others, and they provide ideal alternative sites for night-time activities.

26. Outdoor activities

Children, in particular, have a better sense of place if the urban setting contains play environments that are scaled to their size and are humanised. The physical setting makes a difference in – and directly contributes to – a child's behaviour and willingness to learn acceptable social behaviour. The urban setting can create the right elements to equip the child for his or her role in the community. Children learn through their senses, so a child at play is learning and can gain from the built environment in a positive way.

Good neighbourhood playgrounds can stimulate multi-sensory play if they are well designed and provide for the child's experiential appreciation of his or her urban habitat.

Within the category of planned amenities in the urban setting many familiar forms usually come under the umbrella of landscape architecture, such as:

- fountains, shelters, steps, kiosks, bandstands;
- sports fields and landscaped parks;
- trails along natural features;
- botanical gardens and sanctuaries; and
- playgrounds with swings and paved fountains.

Options for recreational space should include a range for both formal (e.g. organised games) and informal (e.g. play space, parks) use.

The extent of formal recreational space will be determined largely by the available space and official standards, and limited by the ability of the target population to bear the costs. Davidson and Payne (1983) suggest that the following considerations are important for formal areas:

- The recreational facilities should be as central as possible to the areas that they serve, although they need not be in the most valuable area of the project site.
- Easy access is crucial, but a location behind commercial, industrial or public facility areas could be suitable.
- Areas for formal games should be level and suitably surfaced.

Image 7.8 Sites essentially for children

For informal areas, Davidson and Payne (1983) suggest:

- They should be provided on a more pragmatic basis.
- Locating a large number of small open spaces relating to housing clusters or local access roads will be economical and socially acceptable, particularly for the supervision of children from their homes.
- Hardened areas may be desirable for older children, though these must be suitably located so that any activity does not affect other users of the social space.

An important factor in current thinking is the matter of responsibility for the maintenance of outdoor amenities with a view to reduction of public costs. Design proposals should be developed in accordance with prudent economic policy, such as:

- Private maintenance of garden areas in front of houses, which could include the home-owner's responsibility for the maintenance of adjacent street trees.
- Maintenance of sports areas by clubs.
- Maintenance of small public gardens by commercial establishments, such as nearby cafés.

27. Integrate nature

Nature is that part of the world untouched by man, and the remaining pure natural regions should be safeguarded from human intrusion. On the other hand, if human-managed landscapes, such as farmland and forests, are considered part of the natural setting, the city and the inhabited countryside should be considered as a unit. Lynch (1981: 256) observes that "the exploiter (city) and the exploited (countryside) have always been linked together socially, economically and politically."

The integration of natural regimes is not just a matter of saving plants and animals, but of making their presence apparent. "The movements of sun and tides, the cycles of weeds and insects and men, can all be celebrated within the spatial network of the urban setting" (Lynch, 1981: 257). The urban dweller can be liberated from the dichotomies of city and country, artificial and natural, man versus other living things, once the city can be accepted as being as natural as a farm.

The ecological and ecosystem perspectives are providing a common 'language' or set of frameworks across those fields that is facilitating integrative and participatory approaches across disciplines and between design teams and the public, and in the process further reinforcing an

> *ecological worldview. Regenerative development had already begun to shift the old, building-centric definition of the built environment to include the relationships between and among buildings, infrastructure, and natural systems, as well as the culture, economy and politics of communities. Its concept of place-sourced design is providing a means of engaging the will of a community around aligning human and natural communities around shared purposes. Given its holistic and integrative character, it could be anticipated that these more comprehensive applications will be a continuing trend.*
>
> (Mang and Reed, 2012: 28–29)

The integration of natural regimes, in this context, implies the integration of natural resources, which are common property and have a particular place in social wellbeing. Due to pressures on such resources, they must be brought into the management plan for urban settings. The United States Multiple Use/Sustained Yield Act of 1960 "mandated the US Forest Service to recognize 1) the diversity and ecosystemic characteristics of land, and 2) the need to regulate the resource yields of these lands in a way that could be sustained" (Steiner *et al.*, 1988: 31).

Stauth (1983: 93) argues that "the destruction of common property resources may well be [a] more serious problem for society" than pollution, for the following reasons:

- It is a far more insidious phenomenon because it is often a gradual process, the effects are not always so obvious, and the ultimate implications for social wellbeing are far from clear.
- It will probably prove to be a more intractable problem because dealing with it will require much greater sacrifices on the part of society.

The above considerations of the management of natural resources on a sustained yield basis could well require physical space allocations or integration of resource areas into the fabric of the urban setting so that they and the urban dweller are both enriched.

Where development is about to take place, a 'green scorecard' (Chernushenko, 1994) highlights the areas that should be considered in the pre-design process:

- If not the developer, is an agency accountable for environmental costs?
- Will any natural spaces or wilderness be developed?
- Will buildings be expanded into protected natural areas?
- Is an environmental impact assessment needed and has it been prepared?

Image 7.9 Cultural monument sites in nature

- What steps have been taken to protect natural spaces, habitats and/or species?
- What restorative or rehabilitative measures will be taken?
- Will any habitat or species be harmed or eliminated so that it cannot be remedied?
- Will any significant cultural site be affected?
- What steps have been taken to protect such cultural site(s)?
- Have energy and water conservation technologies, waste management measures and energy-efficient principles and building technology guided the design process in a meaningful way?
- What impact will the development have on transportation levels and infrastructure?
- How will any anticipated demand increases be addressed?
- Has public transport been encouraged and infrastructure improved?
- What external environmental cost will there be to service the site with roads and other services?
- What steps have been taken to mitigate external social and environmental costs?
- What steps have been taken to ensure a positive legacy from the development, economically, socially and environmentally, in terms of its sustainability?

These issues of 'greenness' would apply equally to infill development, where 'newcomer' development should show respect for the attributes of the locality and for the preservation of important archaeological and natural imprints.

28. Biogeography

A biogeographical approach to planning is proposed by Roberts (1985), and a return to the data and ideas of biogeographers who have studied species communities on offshore islands is advocated. Whatever the cause of its isolation, one may expect many relationships to remain constant between the biology of an isolated area and its size, shape and remoteness. The equilibrium theory of biogeography has its origins in the work of MacArthur and Wilson in the 1960s. Their hypothesis is that there is a relationship between species richness and island area, distance from colonising source and, in the case of new islands, time. According to the theory, an equilibrium number of species should be found once maturity is reached and immigration rates balance extinction rates.

Although urban growth appears to destroy wildlife habitats and reduce the diversity of flora and fauna, the new buildings, open spaces and food sources in cities provide a great variety of ecological situations that are exploited by certain plants and animals. Within each of these urban habitats an equilibrium develops between the colonising plants and their physical and biological environment (Davis and Glick, 1978).

Image 7.10 Return nature to the city with soft landscaping

"The notion of corridors linking 'habitat islands' together is perhaps one of the more practical uses of island biogeographic theory in urban areas." This approach "should allow for the development of open space networks which are ecologically resilient and diverse, and combine a low cost of maintenance with high scientific, educational, aesthetic and recreational value" (Roberts, 1985: 11). The open space network, including the primary street system, the neighbourhood street and square, and private social spaces, would potentially contribute to the 'linking corridor' concept. The application of such concepts could strengthen the ecological base and encourage species diversity.

Principles for the design of habitat islands in urban areas could be derived from MacArthur and Wilson's (1967) theory for offshore islands. Based on the thesis that nature reserves behave as habitat islands, a set of principles could be employed with the aim of optimising the function that reserves have in saving species. In an adapted form, these principles could be applied to the planning of open spaces in the urban setting, so that they promote species diversity and sustainability. Roberts (1985) summarises this concept as follows:

- A large habitat area is better than a small one for two reasons: the large area can hold more species at equilibrium, and it will have a lower extinction rate.
- Several smaller areas adding up to the total area are not biogeographically equivalent to it, since they tend to support a smaller number of species.
- The equilibrium number of species in one of the smaller habitats can, however, be raised by increasing the immigration rate to it. This can be done by judicious juxtaposition of the several scattered reserves, and by providing corridors of stepping stones of natural habitat between them.
- Any habitat should be as near to circular as other factors permit, to minimise dispersal distances within the habitat. If the habitat area becomes narrowed or has dead-end peninsulas, local extinction rates are likely to be high due to the presence of small populations and peripheral disturbances, and dispersal is unlikely to keep pace with extinction.

Douglas (1983: 107) states that a "capillary rise of saline groundwater may cause salt attack after a structure is completed." Changes in the groundwater conditions under new urban development trigger changes in the hydrological subsurface profile, which in turn can alter the soil's chemical profile. In the planning of new urban settings, it is therefore important to observe subsurface characteristics and to plan to allow a high degree of surface water penetration through measures allowing penetration and incorporating carefully conceived landscaping.

The city modifies the natural energy balance and air circulation through its multiple reflection and absorption patterns, its rough, uneven surfaces, its lack of water and vegetation over many tracts and additional sources of heat and dust generated by human activity. Intensive landscaping and 'greening' policies by both the public and the private sector should be practised to achieve successful urban settings.

To offset these manifestations of the built environment, each one should be considered in the planning of new urban settings. Solutions to these problems require in-depth study, commencing with the identification of the geomorphic characteristics of the original natural site and landforms of the urban setting. A comprehensive approach can then be developed through appropriate mitigative planning, and discretion regarding soft versus hard landscaping.

In a pioneering article, Davis and Glick (1978) advocated:

- A combination of careful planning and benign neglect.
- The need for some abandonment of the 'well-entrenched manicure complex' to ensure that the natural diversity of regenerating nature is not entirely replaced by the uniform and technology-dependent landscape of established design tradition.
- The recognition that urban habitat islands and corridors are biogeographically valuable, as they provide 'reservoirs' and 'stepping-stones' for a variety of plants and animals.

Compared to the traditional park, woodland-like communities may be more expensive to establish initially, but these new natural areas may well prove cheaper in the long run, because they require less maintenance than the traditional mown grass and flower beds of the traditional park (Gerell, 1988).

Only by rethinking planning and indeed management policy can ecological viability and conservation of indigenous flora and fauna be achieved. By ignoring open space resources, biogeographical capabilities of the open space network become limited.

Brady *et al.* (1978) developed a typology for the urban ecosystem and its relationship to larger biogeographical landscape units as a tool for the study of urban ecosystem dynamics. The authors applied this typology specifically to the North American situation, but it could be applied to urban spatial networks in other contexts by adaptation of the terminology for colloquial usage and in turn towards improved integrated environmental management.

29. Geomorphic impacts

In planning the physical change of a new urban setting, a process of geomorphological modification will inevitably take place.

The city is a new landscape, with new forms such as man-made cliffs and long and narrow tracts of hardened surface, sometimes broken by the robust intervention of the original natural landscape. The nature of the land cover has a major effect on climate, wind patterns, nutrient status and diversity of the intra-urban ecosystems (as city habitats and biotic communities may be called). The spectrum of spaces in the urban environment ranges from the completely covered, built-up central business area to relicts of the rural landscape in the form of remnant woodlands, copses, commons and urban heaths.

The hydrological changes associated with urban development cause exposure of the soil during the development of new construction sites, allowing tepid erosion of soils and up to one-hundredfold increases in silt loading in river catchments (Douglas, 1983), thereby also influencing the extent of floodplains. The extraction of ground water by the standard practice of hard channelling of stormwater withholds water from the subsurface, which may create physical changes and induce subsidence and slope instability. In planning new urban environments, the possibility of precipitating mass ground movement must be met with solutions such as lessening hard surfacing and incorporating any relict landforms as far as is practicable.

Legal controls introduced in North Carolina in 1973 to limit the effects of development activities on natural systems require:

- A sediment and erosion control plan for all urban development on areas greater than one acre.
- Re-establishment of cover on disturbed areas inside thirty days if active construction is not proceeding.
- Retention of a buffer strip between the disturbed areas and streams or lakes.
- Grading of cut and fill slopes to a stable angle, and application of vegetation or structural measures within thirty days of slope modification.

Coastal sites are particularly sensitive to change due to the dynamic and complex nature of their forms. Impacts of development affecting estuaries cannot be evaluated simplistically and require specialised study.

Apart from changes to the landform and surfacing in the built environment, Douglas (1983) states that designers and planners must understand that when buildings are grouped together:

- They influence the energy balances of one another and complicate the air movements and heat flows in the intervening spaces.
- The bulk of two buildings of differing size adjacent to each other affects wind flows so strongly that the downward flow of air on the taller block creates higher wind speeds in two zones. Such effects can be avoided by carrying out appropriate analysis at the design stage, if necessary with wind-tunnel models, and thereby determining the spacing to minimise gusting.
- Vertical walls tend to reflect solar radiation towards the ground rather than back to the sky. Re-radiation from the ground bounces back on to the walls of the adjacent buildings. Skyscrapers can absorb more than six times the heat absorbed by the featureless rural plain, but an area of dispersed suburban housing would absorb only slightly more than the rural plain (Terjung, 1982).
- The orientation of the streets and the season of the year may affect the absorption of short-wave radiation.

The intensity, size and shape of any urban heat island varies with the topography of the city, land uses within the city, patterns of artificial heat generation and the weather. The inevitable changes to weather patterns in a region of urban development are well documented. Changes in the chemistry of the rain from the emission of substances into the atmosphere affect geomorphic processes, including building materials. Chemical weathering

Image 7.11 Public park: legacy of mega-sports event

of building materials will be interlinked with any change in the quality of air over urban areas.

30. Benefit–cost rating

Jules Dupuit, a French engineer, first introduced the concept of cost–benefit analysis in the 1930s (Mind Tools, n.d.). It became popular in the 1950s as a simple way of weighing up costs and benefits in order to determine whether to proceed with a project. It is a way of quantitatively determining benefit in relation to cost. This assessment could apply to the allocation of a budget to aspects of an urban placemaking project as well as affordability.

Before committing to ratings in a methodology relating to the attributes of urban social space, practitioners normally undertake a parallel exercise which involves:

- brainstorming all the costs associated with a project;
- assigning a monetary value to the cost of any design or planning action;
- assigning a monetary value to the benefit of such an action; and
- comparing the costs and benefits in order to determine the optimum allocation for the greater benefit.

Applied to the placemaking of urban public space, to meet the spatial performance goals, aesthetics, safety and recreational facilities, for instance, might take precedence over other attributes.

Through the international sports agencies, a new dynamic is helping to shape new or reshape existing urban environments. Mega-sports events funded with public support and sponsored by commercial advertising or the sale of television rights provide the capital for inner-city regenerative projects. The cost of upgrading of a host city environment, normally limited by a tight fiscal budget, is therefore overcome and the after-use legacy is generally impressive.

References

Alexander, C., Ishikawa, S. and Silverstein, M. *A Pattern Language* (New York: Oxford University Press, 1977).

Baker, I., Thompson, J.C. and Bowers, P.H. "Children in Traffic Research on Post-Radburn Housing Areas." *Ekistics* 52(312) (1985): 247–252.

Bentley, I., Alcock, A., Murrain, P., McGlynn, S. and Smith, G. *Responsive Environments: A Manual for Designers* (London: Architectural Press, 1985).

Brady, R.F., Tobias, T., Eagles, P.F., Ohrner, R., Micak, J., Veale, B. and Dorney, R.S. "A Typology for the Urban Ecosystem and its Relationship to Larger Biogeographical Landscape Units." *Urban Ecology* 4 (1978): 11–28.

Caminos, H. and Goethert, R. *Urbanization Primer: Project Assessment, Site Analysis, Design Criteria for Site and Services of Similar Dwelling Environments in Developing Areas* (Cambridge, MA: The MIT Press, 1978).

Chernushenko, D. *Greening Our Games: Running Sports Events and Localities that Won't Cost the Earth* (Ottawa: Canada Centurion Publishing and Marketing, 1994).

Ching, F.D.K. *Architecture, Form, Space and Order* (New York: Van Nostrand Reinhold Co., 1979).

Dantzig, G.B. and Saarty, T.L. *Compact City: A Plan for a Livable Urban Environment* (San Francisco, CA: Freeman and Co., 1973).

Davidson, F. and Payne, G.K. *Urban Projects Manual* (Liverpool: Liverpool University Press, 1983).

Davis, A.M. and Glick, T.F. "Urban Ecosystems and Island Biogeography." *Environmental Conservation* 5(4) (1978): 299–304.

Dewar, D. "Urban Poverty and City Development." *Architecture SA* March/April (1984): 27–28.

Dewar, D. and Uytenbogaardt, R.F. *Housing: A Comparative Evaluation of Urbanism in Cape Town* (Cape Town: Urban Planners Research Unit, 1977).

Doczi, G. *The Power of Limits: Proportional Harmonies in Nature, Art and Architecture* (London: Shambhala, 1985).

Douglas, I. *The Urban Environment* (London: Edward Arnold, 1983).

Gerell, R. "Faunal Diversity and Vegetation Structure of Some Indigenous Forests in Southern Sweden." *Holarctic Ecology* (1988): 87–95.

Eubank-Ahrens, B. "A Closer Look at the Users of *Woonerven.*" In A.V. Moudon (ed.), *Public Streets for Public Use* (New York: Van Nostrand Reinhold Co., 1987).

Gans, H.J. *People and Plans: Essays on Urban Problems and Solutions* (New York: Columbia University Press, 1991).

Gibson, J. *Ecological Approach to Visual Perception* (Boston, MA: Houghton Mifflin, 1987).

Girardet, H. *Gaia Atlas of Cities* (London: Gaia Books, 1992).

Goffman, E. *The Presentation of Self in Everyday Life* (New York: Doubleday, 1959).

Hall, E.T. *The Hidden Dimension, Garden City* (New York: Doubleday, 1966).

Heath, T. *Method in Architecture* (Devon: John Wiley and Sons, 1984).

Hillier, B. and Hanson, J. *The Social Logic of Space* (Cambridge: Cambridge University Press, 1984).

Kidder-Smith, G.E. *Italy Builds* (London: Architectural Press, 1954).

Jacobs, J. *The Death and Life of Great American Cities* (New York: Random House, 1961).

Loeckx, A. *et al. Urban Trialogues: Visions, Projects, Co-productions: Localising Agenda 21* (Nairobi: UN-Habitat, 2004).

Lynch, K. *A Theory of Good City Form* (London: The MIT Press, 1981).
MacArthur, R.E. and Wilson, E.O. *The Theory of Island Biogeography* (Princeton, NJ: Princeton University Press, 1967).
Mang, P. and Reed, W. "Designing from Place: A Regenerative Framework and Methodology." *Building Research and Information* 40(1) (2012): 23–38.
Martin, L. and March, L. *Urban Space and Structures* (Cambridge: Cambridge University Press, 1972).
Mills, G. "Recreating Urban Space." *Architecture SA* July/August (1988): 37–38.
Mind Tools. "Cost–Benefit Analysis: Deciding, Quantitavely, whether to Go ahead" (n.d.). Available at: www.mindtools.com/pages/article/newTED_08.htm, accessed 17 July 2015.
Morkel, M.P. "Residential Densities – Quo Vadis." *Housing in South Africa* December (1988): 21.
Norberg-Schulz, C. *Genus Loci: Towards a Phenomenology of Architecture* (New York: Rizzoli, 1971).
Olbrich, H. (ed.) *Lexikon der Kunst* (Leipzig: Seemann, 1987).
Peck, A.J.A. "Agoric Planning." *Ekistics* 49(295) (1982): 333–336.
Rapoport, A. *Human Aspects of Urban Form* (New York: Pergamon Press, 1977).
Reekie, R.F. *Design in the Built Environment* (London: Edward Arnold, 1972).
Roberts, D. "Urban Open Space Planning in South Africa: The Need for a New Approach." *Environment October/November* (1985): 11–13.
Schuitema, P. *Syst-o-color: Vier-kleurensysteem* (The Hague: Mouton, 1965).
Schumacher, F. "Color in Architecture." In M. Duttmann, F. Schmuck and J. Uhl (eds), *Color in Townscape* (London: The Architectural Press, 1981).
Sitte, C. *City Planning According to Artistic Principles* (London: Phaidon Press, 1965).
Smithson, A. and Smithson, P. *Urban Structuring: Studies of Alison and Peter Smithson* (London and New York: Studio Vista, Reinhold, 1967).
Spirn, A.W. "Better Air Quality at Street Level: Strategies for Urban Design." In A.V. Moudon (ed.), *Public Streets for Public Use* (New York: Van Nostrand Reinhold Co., 1987).
Stauth, R. "Environmental Economics." In R.F. Fuggle and M.A. Rabie (eds), *Environmental Concerns in South Africa* (Cape Town: Juta & Co., 1983).
Steiner, F., Young, G. and Zube, E. "Ecological Planning: Retrospect and Prospect." *Landscape Journal* 7(1) (1988): 31–39.
Sudjic, D. *The Edifice Complex: How the Rich and Powerful Shape the World* (London: Penguin, 2006).
Terjung, W.H. *Process-Response Systems in Physical Geography* (Bonn: Ferd. Dümmlers Verlag, 1982).
Trancik, R. *Finding Lost Space* (New York: Van Nostrand Reinhold Co., 1986).
Tunnard, C. and Pushkarev, B. *Man-made America: Chaos or Control? An Enquiry into Selected Problems of Design in the Urbanised Landscape* (New Haven, CT: Yale University Press, 1963).
Viljoen, H., Van Staden, F., Grieve, K. and Van Deventer, V. *Environmental Psychology: An Introduction* (Johannesburg: Lexicon, 1988).
Wheeler, M. *Roman Art and Architecture* (New York: Praeger, 1964).
Whyte, W.H. "Small Space is Beautiful: Design as if People Mattered." *Technology Review* 85(5) (1982): 36–40.

Conclusion

Practitioners in the urban environment, politicians, corporations, economists, manufacturers and retailers, environmental agencies, religious institutions and all leaders who believe that the 'business as usual' approach remains a viable policy ignore the fact that the world's resources are finite. Current estimates of the world's population stand at around 7 billion people and the largest wave of urban growth in history has recently been recorded. Since 2008, for the first time in history, more than half of the world's population have been living in towns and cities, and by 2030 this number is estimated to swell to 8.5 billion (www.un.org/sustainabledevelopment), with urban growth concentrated in Africa and Asia. One billion people currently live in urban slums, which are typically overcrowded, polluted and dangerous, and where basic services such as clean water and sanitation are absent. Smaller towns and cities have fewer resources to respond to the quantum leap of change.

Ideologies, mindsets often fuelled by self-interest, will come and go, but they are capable of diverting attention away from commitment to a value system which has relevance in the escalating global crisis between humankind and our habitat. For example, a popular theology incorporates a Crusader mindset and draws on ancient scriptures to promote its cause, quoting a passage as a mandate from God for humankind's "dominion over the fish of the sea, and over the fowl of the air, and over the cattle, and over all the earth, and over every creeping thing that creepeth upon the earth" (Genesis 1:26).

However, dominion can be interpreted in many ways, including good stewardship, which in the global context is the only route available for a world facing an escalating scale of challenges in population growth, migration and urbanisation, and an escalating demand for natural resources. The relevance to urban design and planning briefs in the post-millennium era is conclusive – that to avoid costly failure, urban design and planning briefs should be products of democratic engagement with the end-user, the urban dweller.

The ethical imperative in terms of development, lifestyle and consumption is inescapable if the root causes of future resource depletion from the growing energy and water demands are not addressed. In President Barack Obama's words:

> Change will not come if we wait for some other person, or if we wait for some other time. We are the ones we've been waiting for. We are the change that we seek . . . Change is brought about because ordinary people do extraordinary things . . . One voice can change a room, and if one voice can change a room, then it can change a city, and if it can change a city, it can change a state, and if it change a state, it can change a nation, and if it can change a nation, it can change the world. Your voice can change the world.
>
> (Obama, n.d.)

It is interesting to note that excellence in ordering urban space can be achieved through low technology, basic craft skills and the creative drive of the human spirit. Even with minimal technological advancement, vernacular typologies, solutions that responded with honesty to the constraints on resources, were and will remain significant legacies. Born of economic and resource scarcity, the demands of the site, the vicissitudes of climate and the socio-cultural needs not only to survive but to be sustainable, historical vernacular forms were the embodiment of plain common sense. Consider the legacy of traditional urban spaces throughout history, the attributes they possess and what can be learned from them in exhancing the urban experience.

Reference

Obama, B. "Barack Obama Quotes" (n.d.). Available at: www.goodreads.com/author/quotes/6356.Barack_Obama, accessed 10 October 2015.

Appendix 1: Polling sheet (1)

PRO FORMA POLLING SHEET FOR WEIGHTING SCORES
(End-users on the Weighting Panel)

Specific to: ....(urban space component)

Notes:
Scores should reflect the importance of each of the listed spatial performance goals (SPGs) individually by consideration of the extent to which each of the aspects is significant to the member's/members' analyses of the project.

Importance weightings can reflect both positive and negative influences on the SPGs, which in turn will inform the planning primers (PPs).

Scores will be transferred to the Weighting Matrix by the Coordinating Body.

Value in terms of importance to you as end-user	*Spatial Performance Goals (SPGs)*	*Weighting (standardised) 1 (low) to 5 (high)*
I SOCIAL ENCOUNTER Opportunity to meet others	• Open space which is continuous • Pedestrians-only area • Well-used pedestrian space • Places to linger away from crowds and vehicles • Well-planned space for social mingling • Shelter from sun and wind	
II AESTHETIC APPEAL Visually attractive	• Provide sense of place • Well-planned space with character • The use of colour, texture and lighting • Controlled noise level • Neat/orderly appearance • Human-related scale of the space or amenities	

(continued)

(continued)

Value in terms of importance to you as end-user	*Spatial Performance Goals (SPGs)*	*Weighting (standardised) 1 (low) to 5 (high)*
III IDENTITY Self-identity Cultural identity	• Familiar with cognitive association • Specific to cultural identity • Promotes sense of collective ownership • Promotes way of life • A site for cultural symbols, which express the past, present and future	
IV FUNCTIONALITY Serves urban living effectively	• Allows efficient mobility • Access to public transport • Allows efficient access • Vehicular traffic and pedestrian safety • Efficient mixed use of urban space • Proximity between residence, amenities and institutions	
V SOCIAL AMENITY VALUE Socially useful place	• Useful for multiple social activities • Enables social choices • Extends the outdoor function of the private dwelling • Close proximity to residential areas	
VI PRIVACY Freedom from public realm	• Offers escape from urban stress • Serves private territorial needs • Provides transition between private and public needs • Provides transition between neighbourhood and public activities	
VII SAFETY Free from danger and pollution	• Free of vehicular traffic • Safe mobility • Clean air • Secure from urban crime • Physical safety	
VIII ECONOMIC OPPORTUNITY Options to trade or shop	• Option to trade formally or informally • Proximity between residence, business and shops • Nodes to concentrate social activity • Intersections for commercial activity	

Value in terms of importance to you as end-user	*Spatial Performance Goals (SPGs)*	*Weighting (standardised) 1 (low) to 5 (high)*
IX ENTERTAINMENT AND RECREATIONAL OPPORTUNITY Choice of active or passive relaxation	• Provide formal facilities • Provide informal facilities • Allow choice for active or non-active usage	
X ECOLOGICAL DIVERSITY AND NATURE Enrich urban life through contact with nature	• Conserve the natural regimes • Provide formal or informal urban gardens • Foster bird and animal life • Landscape with trees, shrubs and plants • Hard landscape for outdoor activities	

Appendix 2: Polling sheet (2)

PRO FORMA FOR RATING SCORES (Specialists on Rating Panel)
Specific to: ....(urban space component)

Notes:
Scores should reflect the importance of each of the listed spatial performance goals (SPGs) individually and evaluated in the various area(s) of specialisation on the Rating Panel.

Importance ratings can reflect both positive and negative influences on SPGs and planning primers (PPs).

Scores will be transferred to the Rating Matrix by the Coordinating Body.

Spatial performance goals (SPGs) perceived as important to the end-users	*Planning primers (PPs): parameters to inform urban design and planning briefs*	*Ratings (standardised) 1 (low) to 5 (high) or Ratings (non-standardised)*
I SOCIAL ENCOUNTER Opportunity to meet others	• Plan social space for continuity with other urban functions • Plan nodes of pedestrian mingling • Allocate pedestrian-only streets • Allocate places to linger away from crowds and vehicles • Plan for shelter from sun and wind	
II AESTHETIC APPEAL Visual appeal	• Use appropriate colour, texture and lighting • Design space that stimulates • Control spatial proportions relative to peripheral elements • Consider human-related scale of space and amenity • Plan visually legible space • Structure space for potential usage • Enhance sense of place	

Spatial performance goals (SPGs) perceived as important to the end-users	*Planning primers (PPs): parameters to inform urban design and planning briefs*	*Ratings (standardised) 1 (low) to 5 (high) or Ratings (non-standardised)*
III IDENTITY Self-identity Cultural identity	• Recognise cognitive associations with place and cultural symbolism • Design to promote cultural identity	
IV FUNCTIONALITY Serves urban living effectively	• Provide for easy access from residence, other amenities and institutions • Provide access to public transport • Optimise density of human and motor traffic • Explore and strengthen interface with surrounding buildings	
V SOCIAL AMENITY VALUE Socially useful place	• Accessible for wide social activities • Enable sense of ownership	
VI PRIVACY Freedom from public realm	• Plan for neighbourhood scale • Provide transition between neighbourhood and public activities • Recognise private territorial needs	
VII SAFETY Free from danger and pollution	• Separate vehicular traffic to limit pollution • Provide measures for monitoring of urban crime	
VIII ECONOMIC OPPORTUNITY Options to trade or shop	• Allocate site(s) for formal or informal trading • Allow nodal space configuration to concentrate social and commercial activity	
IX ENTERTAINMENT AND RECREATIONAL OPPORTUNITY Choice of active or passive relaxation	• Plan site(s) for formal and informal entertainment and recreational activity	

(continued)

(continued)

Spatial performance goals (SPGs) perceived as important to the end-users	*Planning primers (PPs): parameters to inform urban design and planning briefs*	*Ratings (standardised) 1 (low) to 5 (high) or Ratings (non-standardised)*
X ECOLOGICAL DIVERSITY AND NATURE Enrich urban life through contact with nature	• Conserve and integrate the natural regimes • Provide formal or informal urban gardens to promote biodiversity • Foster bird and animal life • Landscape with trees, shrubs and plants • Accept the existing topography, and design to avoid negative impacts on the natural terrain of the site(s)	
BENEFIT–COST RATIO	• Negotiate realistic budgets to meet SPGs	

Appendix 3: Environmental specifications

Environmental awareness

The Contractor shall ensure that all his staff and subcontractors and their staff attend the Environmental Awareness workshop that will be conducted by the Environmental Consultant before the start of construction.

Principal Agent's brief

- Ensure that the environmental performance is monitored by a designated environmental professional/consultant.
- Ensure that a summary of the environmental performance with regard to the environmental specifications is submitted to the Environmental Consultant as part of a monthly report on the project.
- Ensure that the Contractor implements the recommendations made by the Environmental Consultant.

The Environmental Consultant's brief

- Monitor and evaluate compliance with the specifications.
- Issue regular reports to the Principal Agent in regard to any contraventions of the environmental specifications.
- Agree remedial action and the time-frame for implementation with the Principal Agent.
- Brief the Contractor's staff about the environmental specifications.
- Provide professional advice to the Principal Agent in respect of implementing the environmental specifications.
- Attend site meetings on a when-required basis, and monitor the performance in terms of the environmental specifications.
- Provide recommendations for improving the performance of the Contractor in respect of the environmental specifications.
- Ensure these recommendations are implemented.
- Advise the Principal Agent where adequate standards in terms of the environmental specifications are not being achieved and what remedial action is required.

- Be responsible for producing a comprehensive report at the end of the project, in which the environmental performance of the construction phase is recorded.

Site establishment and management layout plans

- The Contractor is responsible for providing layout plans of the construction site which indicate the following demarcated areas. The plan must be approved by the Principal Agent in consultation with the Environmental Consultant before site establishment is commenced:
  - Planned access and circulation routes.
  - Topsoil and subsoil stockpiles.
  - Working areas.
  - Contractor's camp.
  - Storage areas.
  - Waste collection facilities.
  - Ablution facilities.
  - Stormwater control measures.
  - Buffer zones.
  - Significant features (e.g. cultural and natural) not to be disturbed.
- Access routes and haul roads must be demarcated and vehicle movement to be confined to these roads.
- Excavated areas must be cordoned off and well marked to ensure public safety.
- Construction activities to be restricted according to that designated on the aforementioned plan.
- Materials: topsoil, building materials, waste, etc. must be stored in areas in accordance with the aforementioned plan.
- Site preparation and clearing is to be restricted to the areas designated on the layout plan.
- Physical measures to prevent degradation of soil and water to be marked on the aforementioned plan.

Topsoil

- The Contractor to ensure that the topsoil and subsoil are stockpiled as directed by the Principal Agent and the Environmental Consultant.
- Topsoil to be stripped from the areas indicated below as a first step in establishing the site:
  - Roads.
  - Storage areas including those designated for stockpiling of topsoil.
  - Areas designated for the storage of spoil.
  - Areas which could be polluted by any aspect of construction activity.

- Topsoil to be stripped to a depth as directed by the Engineer.
- The Contractor to ensure that topsoil and subsoil are not mixed during stripping, excavation, stockpiling, reinstatement and rehabilitation of the site.
- Topsoil/subsoil to be protected from wind and rain erosion.
- Both topsoil and subsoil stockpiles shall be kept clear of weeds. The use of chemicals to control weeds not to be permitted.

Rivers, streams, wetlands and other water bodies

- Provision of buffer zones to be made by the Contractor between construction activities and any natural water bodies, rivers or streams in accordance with the layout plan.
- Natural water sources not to be used for the purposes of washing of clothes or vehicles or bathing by site staff.
- Natural water sources not to be used for construction activities such as for the mixing of cement or washing of equipment unless agreed by the Environmental Consultant and the relevant authority.
- The Contractor shall not in any way modify or damage the banks of streams, rivers or natural water bodies.
- Litter and silt traps to be provided by the Contractor as determined by the Environmental Consultant.

Stormwater control

- Natural runoff to be diverted around the site workings to prevent its pollution and routed to the nearest runoff course.
- Stormwater control measures to be implemented in accordance with the requirements of the Environmental Consultant. These may include cross- and side-drains on access and haul roads.
- Where stormwater retention ponds are included in the development plans for the site, these should be constructed in the initial construction phase for stormwater control purposes.
- Where stormwater has accumulated in workings and needs to be pumped out, it should be disposed of in a manner to be approved by the Environmental Consultant. This means that the Contractor is to be responsible for having water tested in accordance with the Environmental Consultant's requirements to establish whether it is contaminated and specialised handling and disposal are necessitated.

Soil erosion

- Measures to prevent erosion of bare soil, excavated areas and soil stockpiles shall be implemented in accordance with the specifications of the Environmental Consultant.

Control of damage to fauna and flora

- The Contractor to ensure that areas designated on the layout plan as being of ecological importance are not to be disturbed.
- A buffer zone shall be established between construction activities and areas of ecological importance as designated by the Environmental Consultant.
- Faunal species only to be removed from the site with the permission of the Environmental Consultant.
- The Contractor to facilitate access to the site for the purposes of relocating plant/animal species prior to the commencement of the clearing of site activities.

Air quality

- Dust: the Contractor to ensure that control measures are applied to minimise dust, particularly in the windy season.
- Engine, machine and other crude oil products may not be used to control dust.
- Emissions: the Contractor to ensure that all vehicles and machinery (such as diesel generators) are well maintained to minimise exhaust emissions.

Waste management: general principles

- Wherever possible waste that is recyclable to be recycled.
- Waste that requires disposal to be disposed of at a licensed landfill site either by the Contractor or by an approved waste removal contractor.
- Illegal dumping not to be tolerated under any circumstances.
- Waste storage facilities to be positioned on site so as to minimise public nuisance.
- Containers for different types of waste to be clearly marked. Minimum of four containers required: recyclables (glass, paper, cardboard, plastic and metal); construction waste; domestic waste; and hazardous waste.
- No burning of waste on site to be permitted.
- No disposal of waste on site, other than that agreed by the Environmental Consultant (such as compostibles and rubble) that may be disposed of on site.
- The Contractor to ensure that no windblown litter occurs.
- The Contractor to notify the Principal Agent in the event of any spills of fuels, chemicals or other hazardous substances that occur on site during the transport of materials to or from the site. Clean-up costs to be for the account of the Contractor. If specialist advice is required to determine clean-up requirements, these to be for the account of the Contractor.

Construction waste

- All clean construction waste (rubble, cement bags, waste cement, wire, nails and timber) to be collected and stored in the appropriate container.
- If material is required for landscaping purposes, construction rubble may be used with the agreement of the Environmental Consultant and stockpiled in a suitable place as directed.
- Wherever possible construction waste that is not used to be recycled, with the emphasis on the opportunities for reuse by the informal sector or by the local authority.

Domestic and office waste

- The construction site to be kept tidy and free of litter at all times.
- Recycling of glass, paper, cardboard and metal is a minimum requirement.
- The Contractor to dispose of these waste products either by sale (e.g. to the small enterprise sector) or make them available to local communities or schools in order that they may generate income from these sources.
- The Contractor to be responsible for establishing an area for composting, as designated by the Environmental Consultant, where organic waste may be placed. The compost to be available for use in revegetation of the site or for use in community landscaping or other projects.

Hazardous waste

- The Contractor to be familiar with those wastes that are legally defined as hazardous and potentially injurious to health. Hazardous wastes are usually proven to be toxic, flammable, explosive, carcinogenic, poisonous or radioactive.
- To be stored in an appropriate container which is to be clearly marked as a hazardous waste container.
- The Contractor to ensure that all potentially hazardous waste is removed and disposed of by an approved hazardous waste contractor.
- Potentially hazardous raw and waste materials to be handled in accordance with the manufacturer's specifications, legal requirements and specifications given on the Material Safety Data Sheet, where available.

Waste water: effluent

- Effluent may not be disposed of into stormwater drains, streams, rivers or any other water body unless agreed by the Environmental Consultant.
- Care to be taken in the washing of vehicles, particularly cement washings, to ensure that these do not enter stormwater systems, streams or wetlands.

Sewage

- Ablution facilities shall be maintained in good working order at all times.
- If sewage facilities are not connected to a reticulated system, the Contractor to ensure that it is removed on a regular basis by an approved contractor or by the relevant local authority.
- The Contractor to ensure that pollution of surface and groundwater resources is prevented.

Noise

- The Contractor to ensure that all equipment complies with the manufacturer's noise level specification. This means that equipment to be maintained and tested.
- Silencer units on plant and vehicles shall be maintained in good working order.
- The Contractor to ensure that all employees wear the appropriate noise gear when working in the vicinity of noisy equipment.
- The Contractor to notify the Principal Agent should it be necessary for construction activities to extend beyond given and agreed times, weekdays, Saturdays, Sundays and Public Holidays.
- The Contractor with the Principal Agent/Environmental Consultant to consult with residents located in the environs of the site should construction activity need to exceed into overtime hours agreed as above.

Lighting

- Lighting of the site to be adequate for safety purposes but not to be intrusive for neighbours.
- Should overtime be necessitated, the Contractor to be responsible for ensuring that the associated lighting does not cause a disturbance to neighbours.

Public safety

- The Contractor to ensure compliance with the requirements of the relevant safety legislation in force in specific locations.
- The Contractor to cordon off excavations and render them clearly visible.
- The Contractor to ensure that due care is taken when heavy vehicles or equipment enter public access roads.
- The Contractor to make appropriate provision for public liability insurance cover.

Community relations

- The Principal Agent and the Environmental Consultant to assist in liaison with the neighbouring community. The Contractor to be responsible for providing information that may be required by the Principal Agent/Environmental Consultant. This could include project schedule, access routes, unsafe areas, etc.
- The Contractor to liaise with the Principal Agent/Environmental Consultant in regard to specific activities that could cause inconvenience to neighbours (such as overtime work, disruption of services). Appropriate notification needs to be done timeously before such activities are carried out.
- The Contractor to make staff available for any formal consultation with affected parties for the purposes of explaining the construction process and to answer queries and/or complaints.

Third-party or public complaints

- The Contractor is responsible for assisting the Principal Agent/ Environmental Consultant with response to queries and/or complaints.
- The Contractor to notify the Principal Agent regarding complaints.
- The Contractor is responsible for undertaking any remedial action as regards complaints, and as required by the Principal Agent/Environmental Consultant.

Site rehabilitation

- The Contractor to rehabilitate the site as required by the Principal Agent/Environmental Consultant.
- Rehabilitation of the original site to an acceptable level prior to any formal landscaping activities to be undertaken by an appropriate contractor approved by the Principal Agent in consultation with the Environmental Consultant.

Source

Olympic Assessment Team. *Strategic Environmental Assessment of the Cape Town Olympic Bid*, Specialist Report No. 3 (Cape Town: Olympic Bid Company, 1997).

Appendix 4: Online references sourced from the internet

Consultative Committee on Urban Ecology. "Aarhus: Demonstrating Ways of Meeting Urban Ecological Renewal Needs." Available at: http://infohouse.p2ric.org/ref/24/23445.htm, accessed 27 November 2015.

McDonald's Corporation. "McDonald's Happy Meal Toy Safety Facts." Available at: www.mcdonalds.com/corp/about/factsheets.html, accessed 19 July 2008.

Project for Public Spaces (PPS). "Strategies for Transforming Cities and Public Spaces through Placemaking." Available at: www.pps.org/reference/ten-strategies-for-transforming-cities-through-placemaking-public-spaces/, accessed 15 June 2015.

Project for Public Spaces (PPS). "Streets as Places: How Transportation Can Create a Sense of Community." Available at: www.pps.org/reference/streets-as-places-how-transportation-can-create-a-sense-of-community/, accessed 19 July 2015.

Project for Public Spaces (PPS). "Qualities of a Great Street." Available at: www.pps.org/reference/qualitiesofagreatstreet/, accessed 19 July 2015.

Project for Public Spaces (PPS). "Placemaking and the Future of Cities." Available at: www.pps.org/reference/placemaking-and-the-future-of-cities/, accessed 19 July 2015.

Project for Public Spaces (PPS). "Reimagining Our Streets as Places: From Transit Routes to Community Roots." Available at: www.pps.org/reference/reimagining-our-streets-as-places-from-transit-routes-to-community-roots/, accessed 19 July 2015.

Project for Public Spaces (PPS). "Placemaking and Place-led Development: A New Paradigm for Cities of the Future." Available at: www.pps.org/reference/placemaking-and-place-led-development-a-new-paradigm-for-cities-of-the-future/, accessed 19 July 2015.

Project for Public Spaces (PPS). "Places in the Making." Department of Urban Studies and Planning at the Massachusetts Institute of Technology (MIT). Available at: www.pps.org/reference/places-in-the-making-mit-report-highlights-the-virtuous-cycle-of-placemaking/, accessed 15 June 2015.

UN-Habitat for a Better Urban Future. "Streets as Public Spaces and Drivers of Urban Prosperity." Available at: http://unhabitat.org/books/streets-as-public-spaces-and-drivers-of-urban-prosperity/, accessed 21 June 2015.

UN-Habitat for a Better Urban Future. "Global Urban Observatory's Research and Technical Team." Available at: http://unhabitat.org/the-relevance-of-street-patterns-and-public-space-in-urban-areas/, accessed 1 June 2015.

UN-Habitat for a Better Urban Future. "The Relevance of Street Patterns and Public Space in Urban Areas." Available at: http://unhabitat.org/the-relevance-of-street-patterns-and-public-space-in-urban-areas/, accessed 1 June 2015.

UN-Habitat for a Better Urban Future. "Streets as Tools for Urban Transformation in Slums: A Street-led Approach to Citywide Slum Upgrading." Available at: http://unhabitat.org/street-led-city-wide-slum-upgrading-claudio-acioly-un-habitat/, accessed 1 June 2015.

UN-Habitat for a Better Urban Future. "Visioning as a Participatory Planning Tool." Available at: http://led.co.za/sites/default/files/cabinet/orgname-raw/document/2012/better_cities_for_all.pdf, accessed 30 November 2015.

UN-Habitat for a Better Urban Future. "Rethinking Public Spaces." Available at: http://unhabitat.org/urban-themes/planning-and-design/, accessed 20 May 2015.

Index

Note: Page numbers followed by 'f' refer to figures and followed by 'i' refer to images.